WINE COLORING BOOK

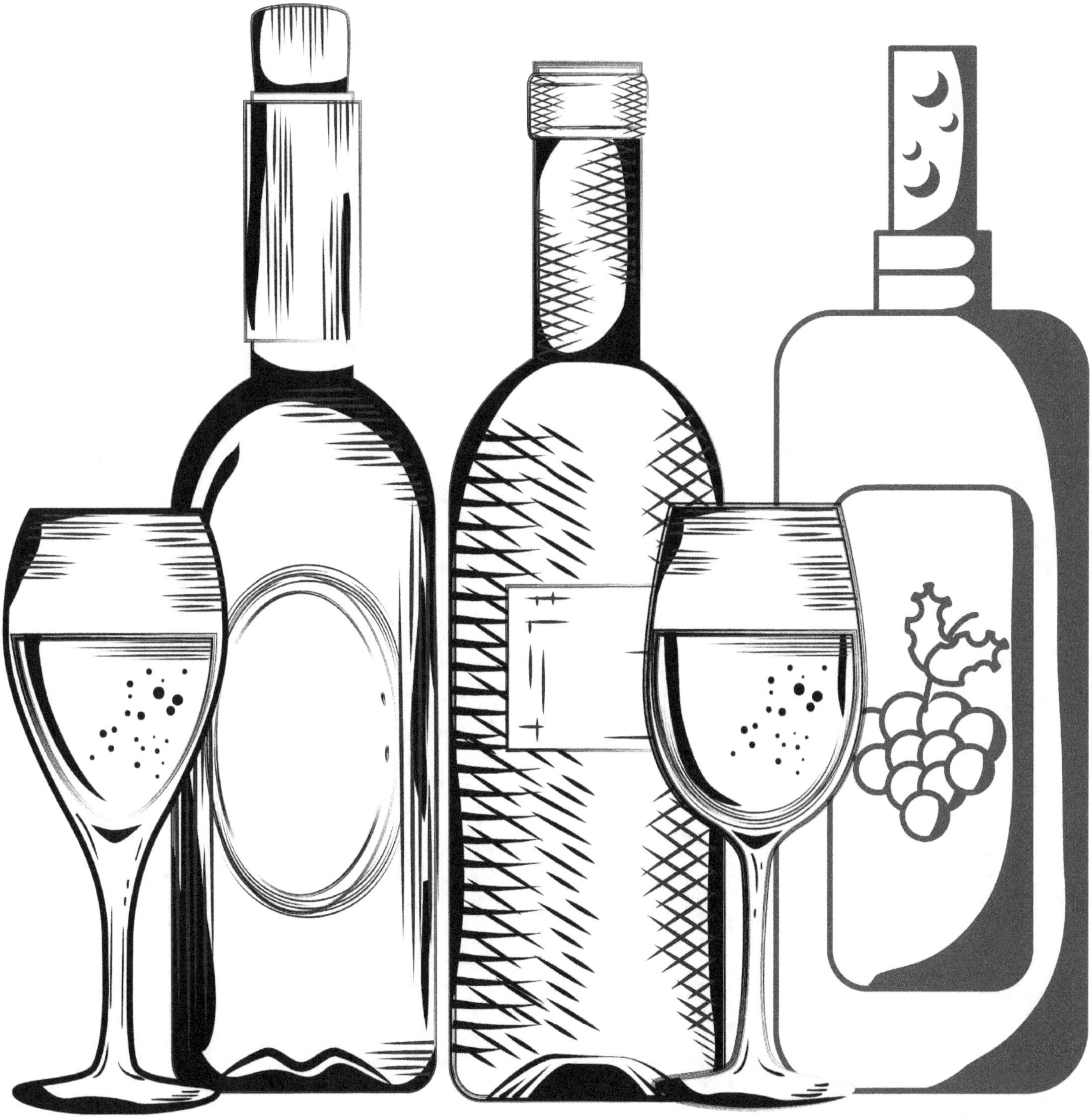

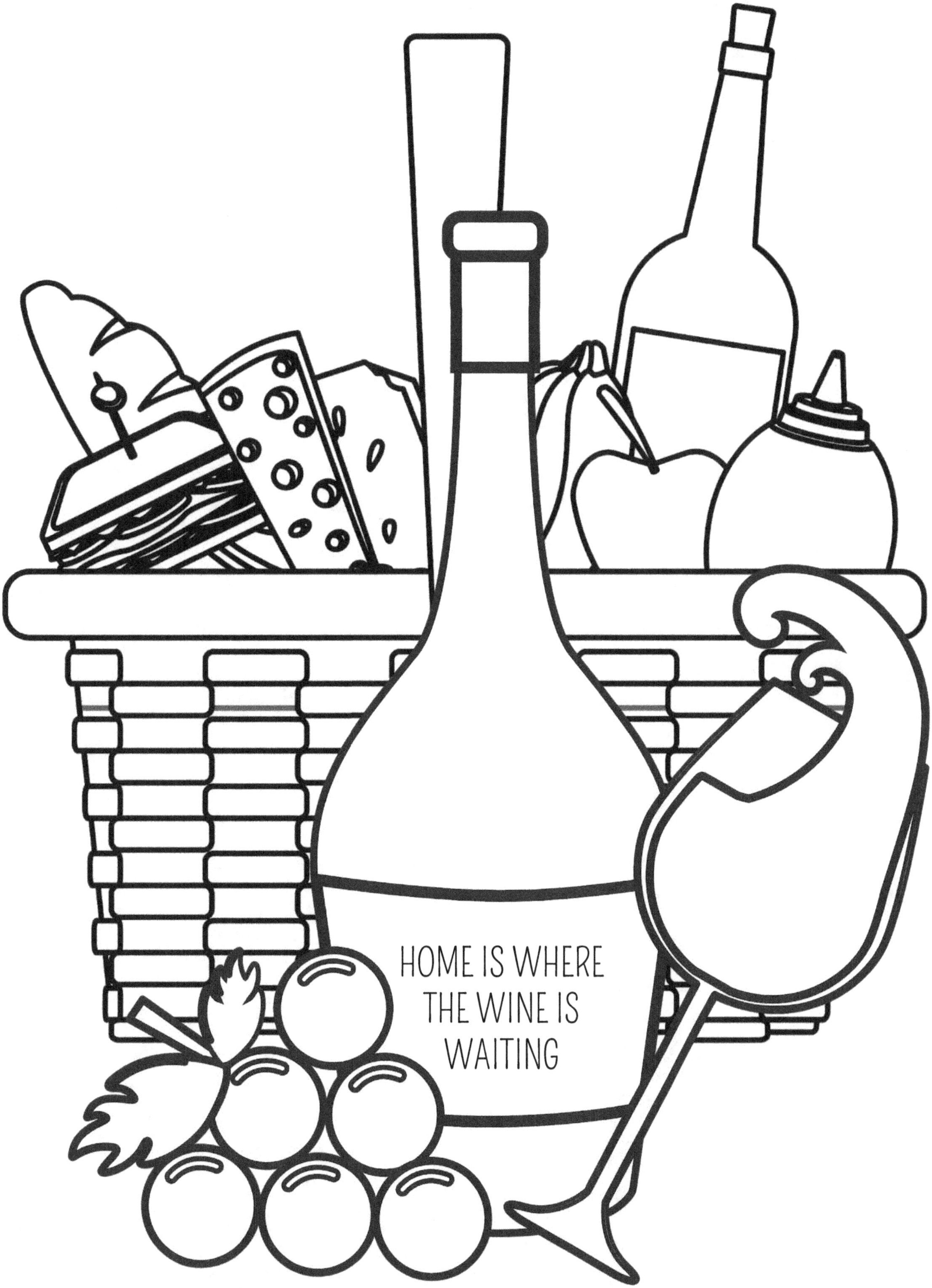
HOME IS WHERE
THE WINE IS
WAITING

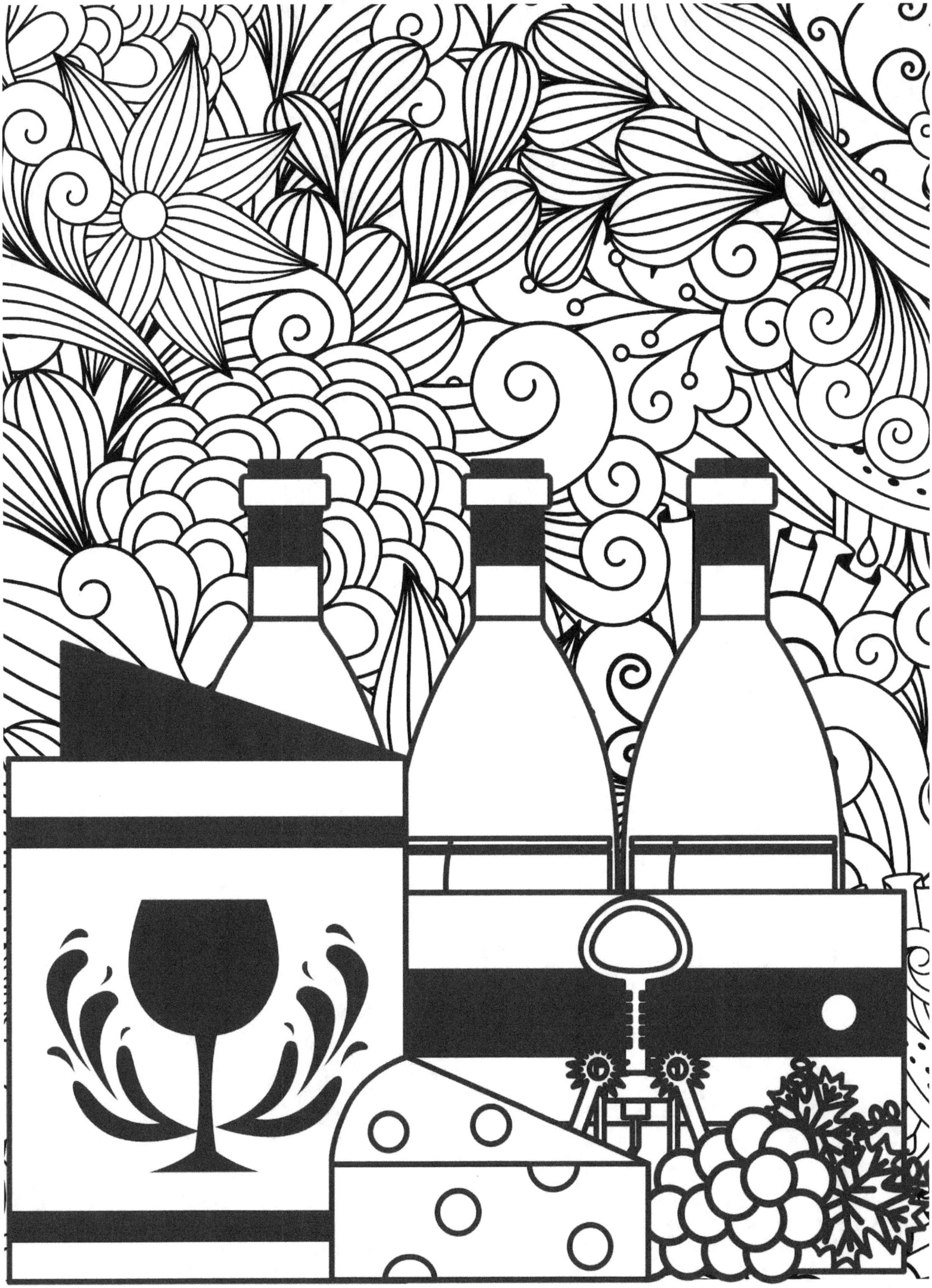

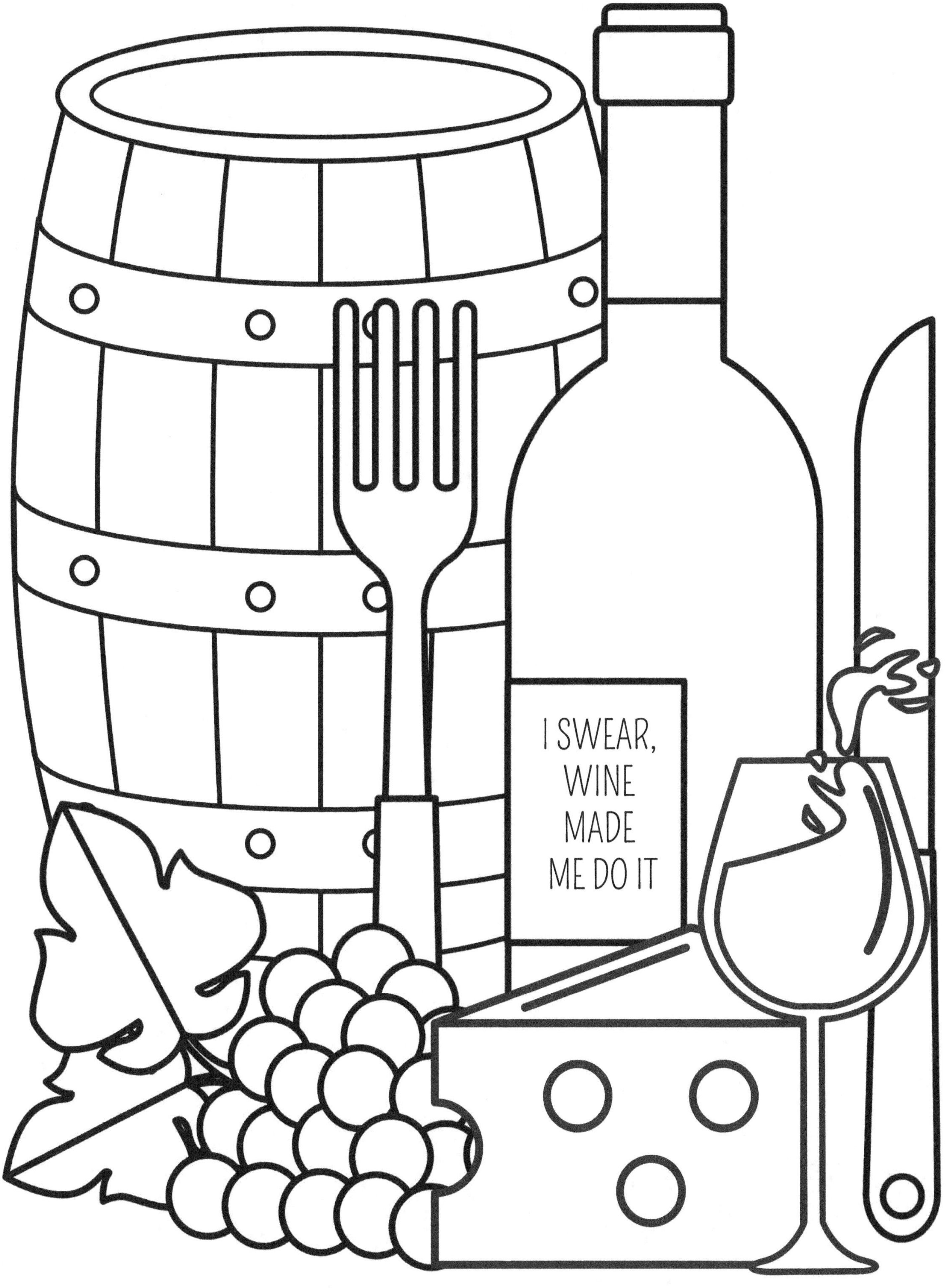
I SWEAR,
WINE
MADE
ME DO IT

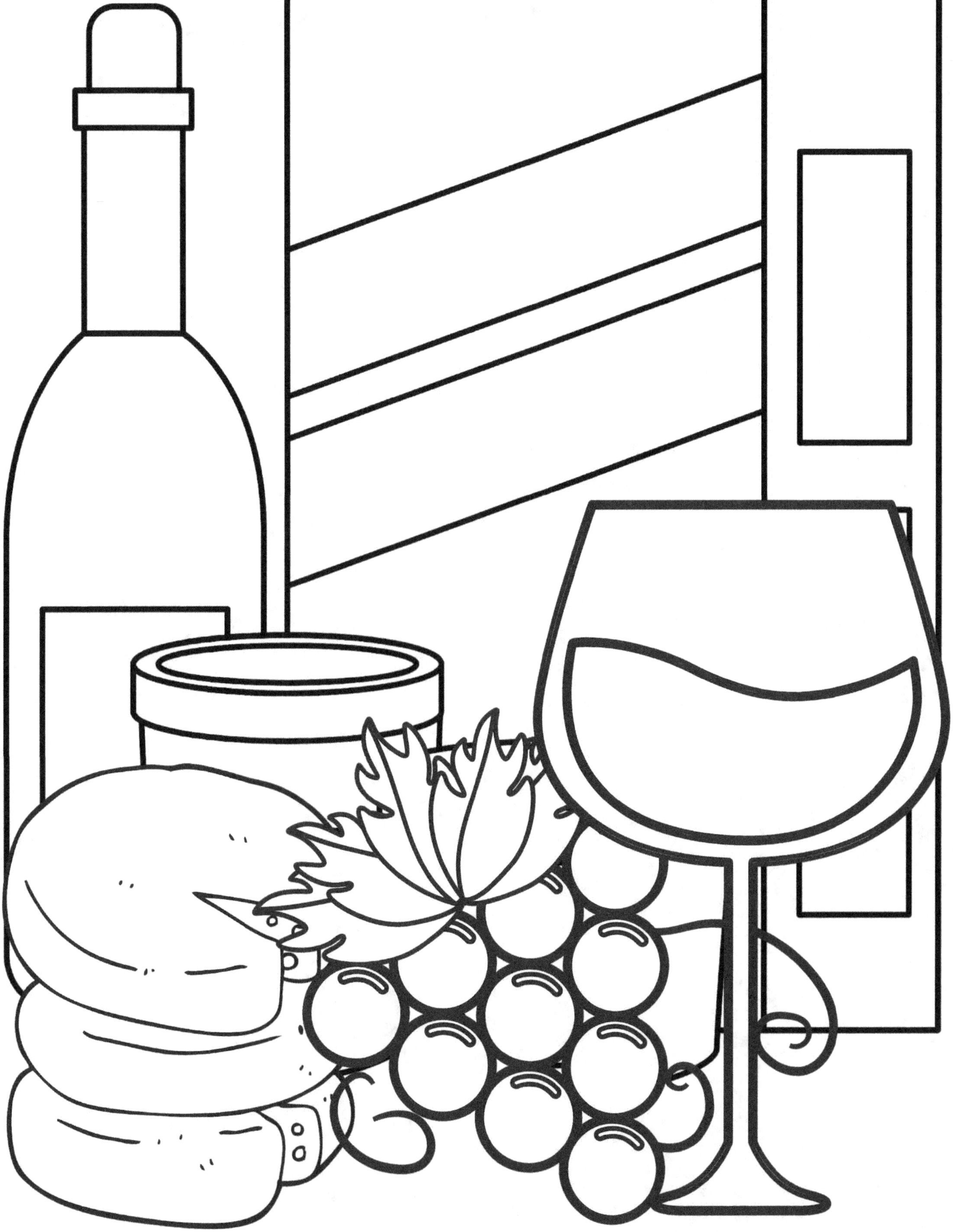

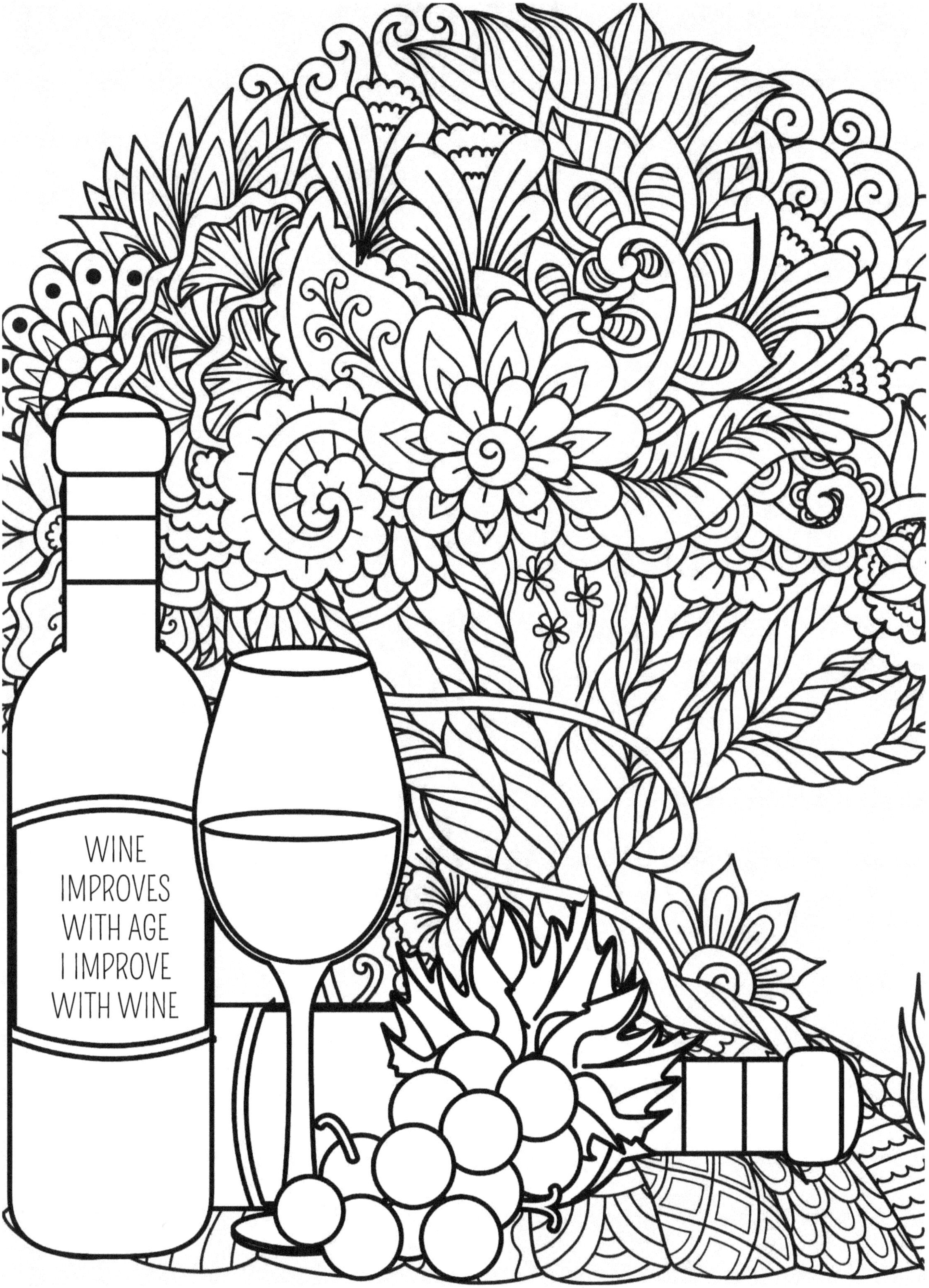
WINE
IMPROVES
WITH AGE
I IMPROVE
WITH WINE

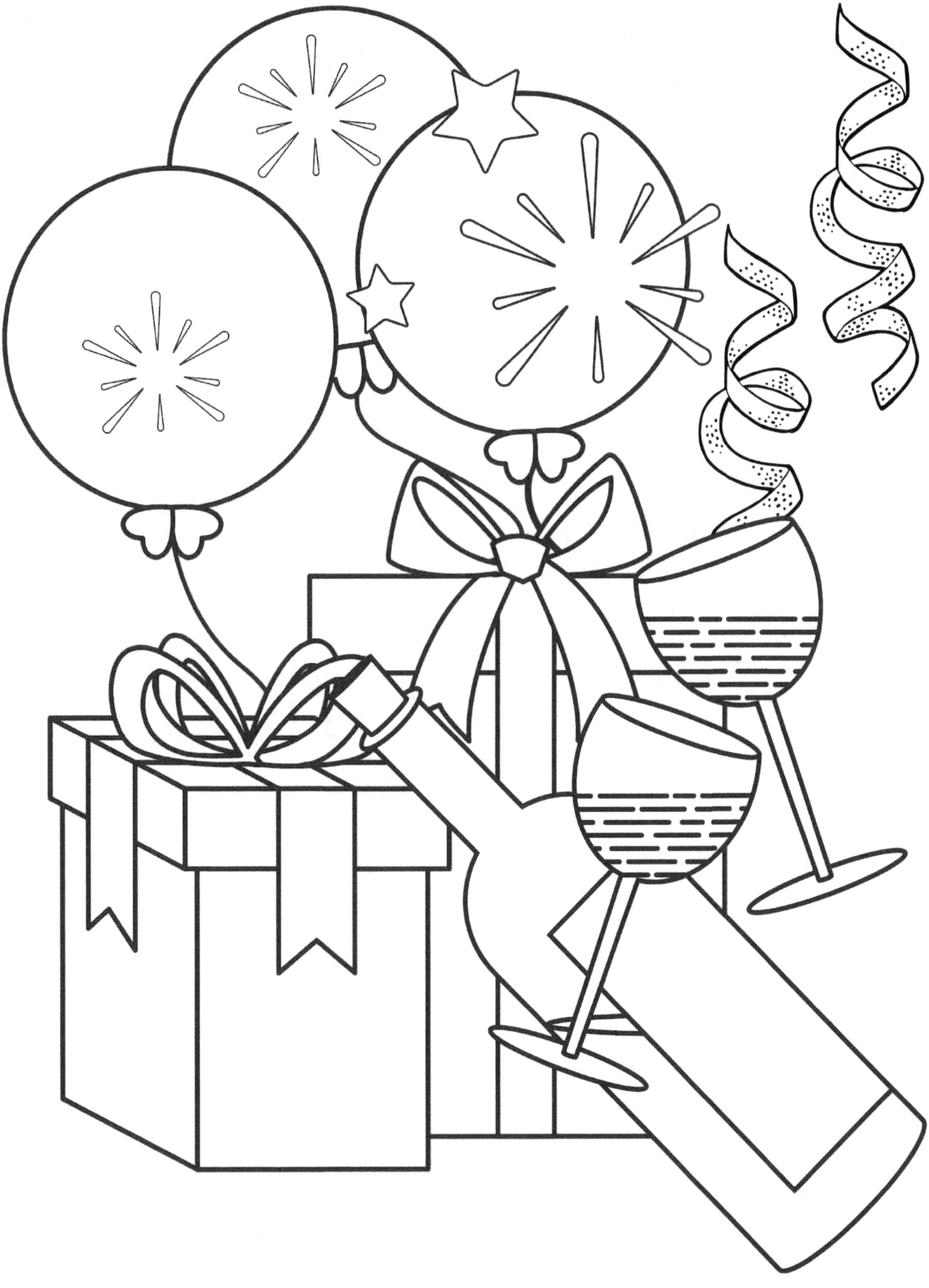

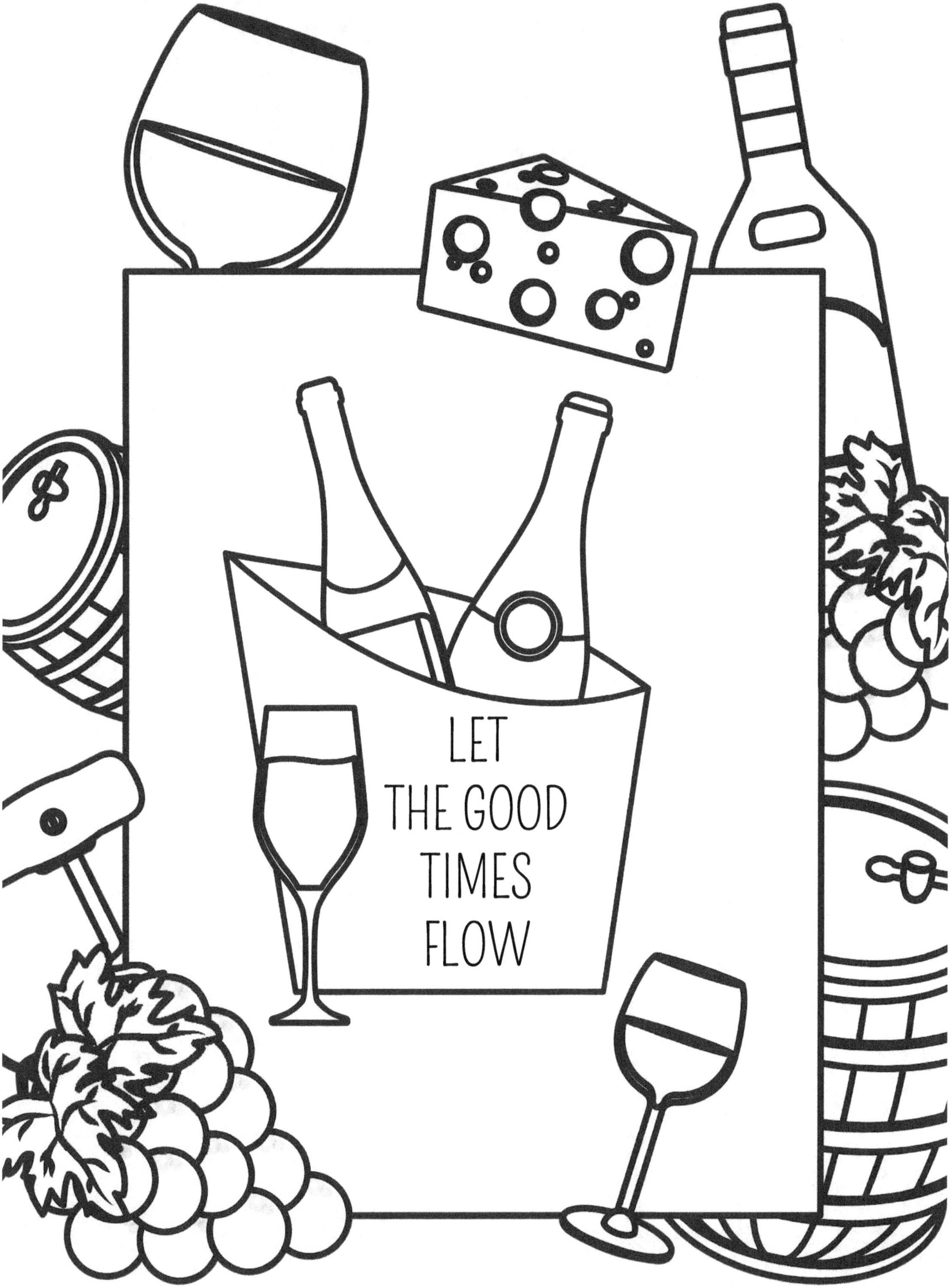
LET
THE GOOD
TIMES
FLOW

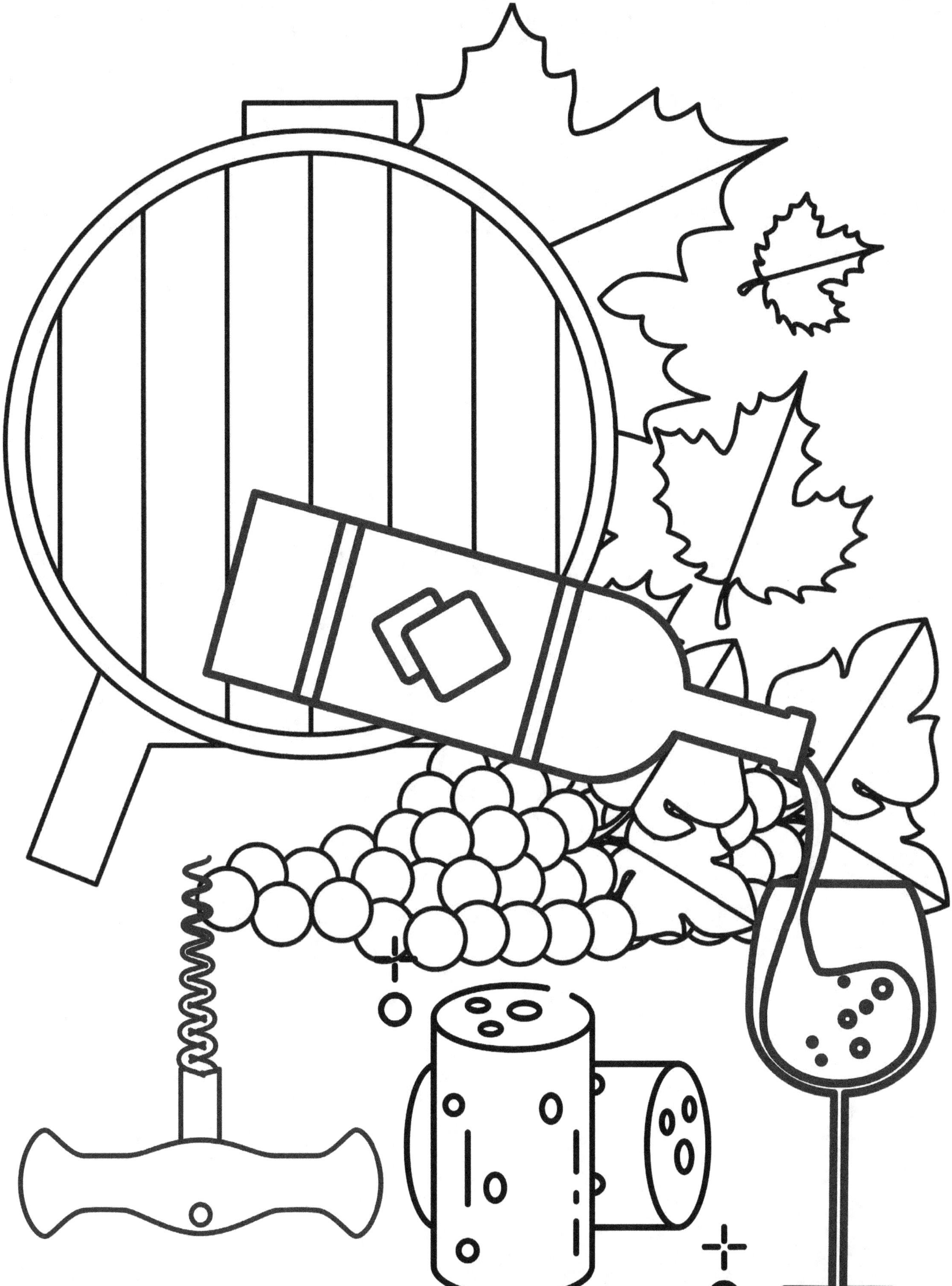

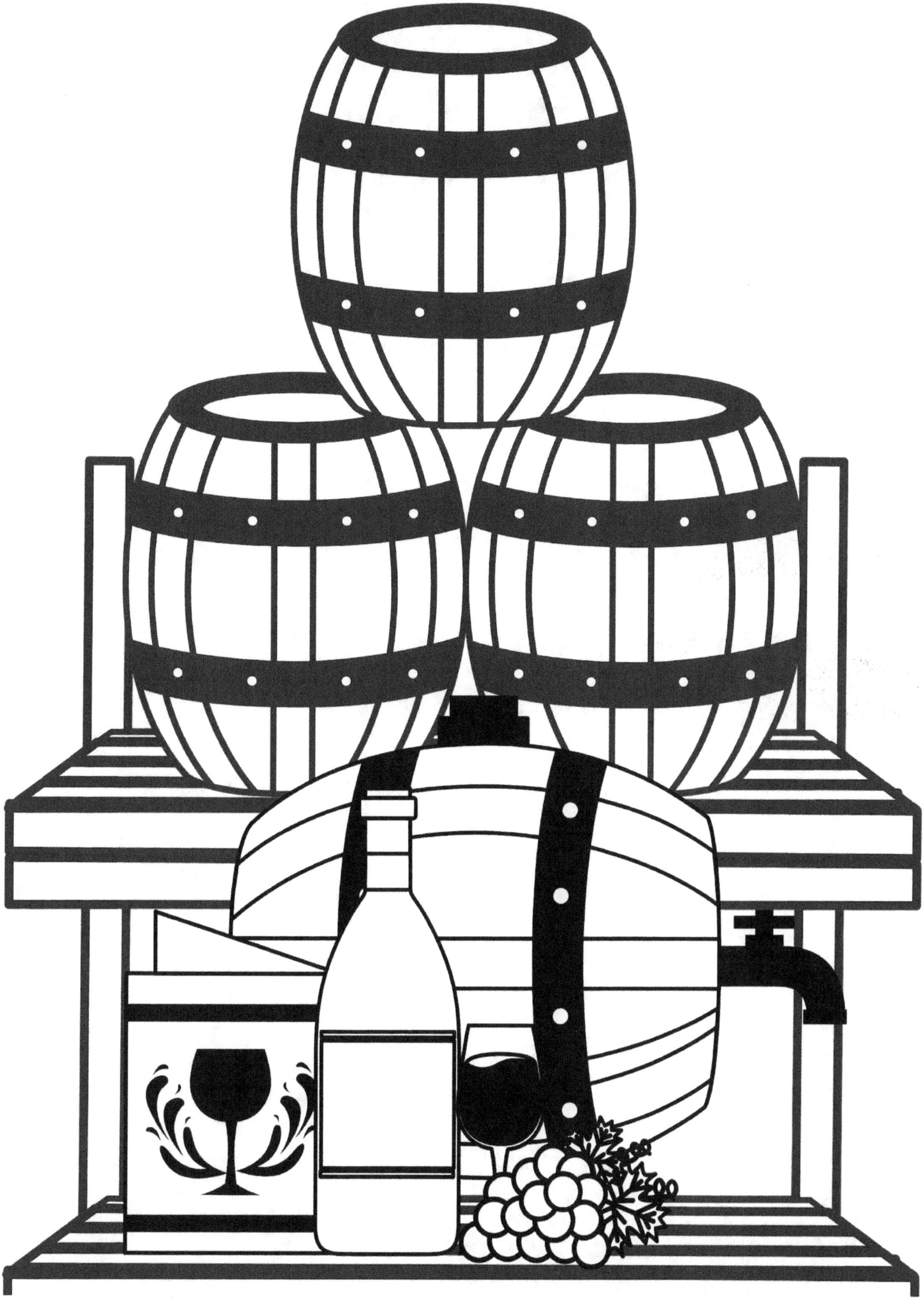

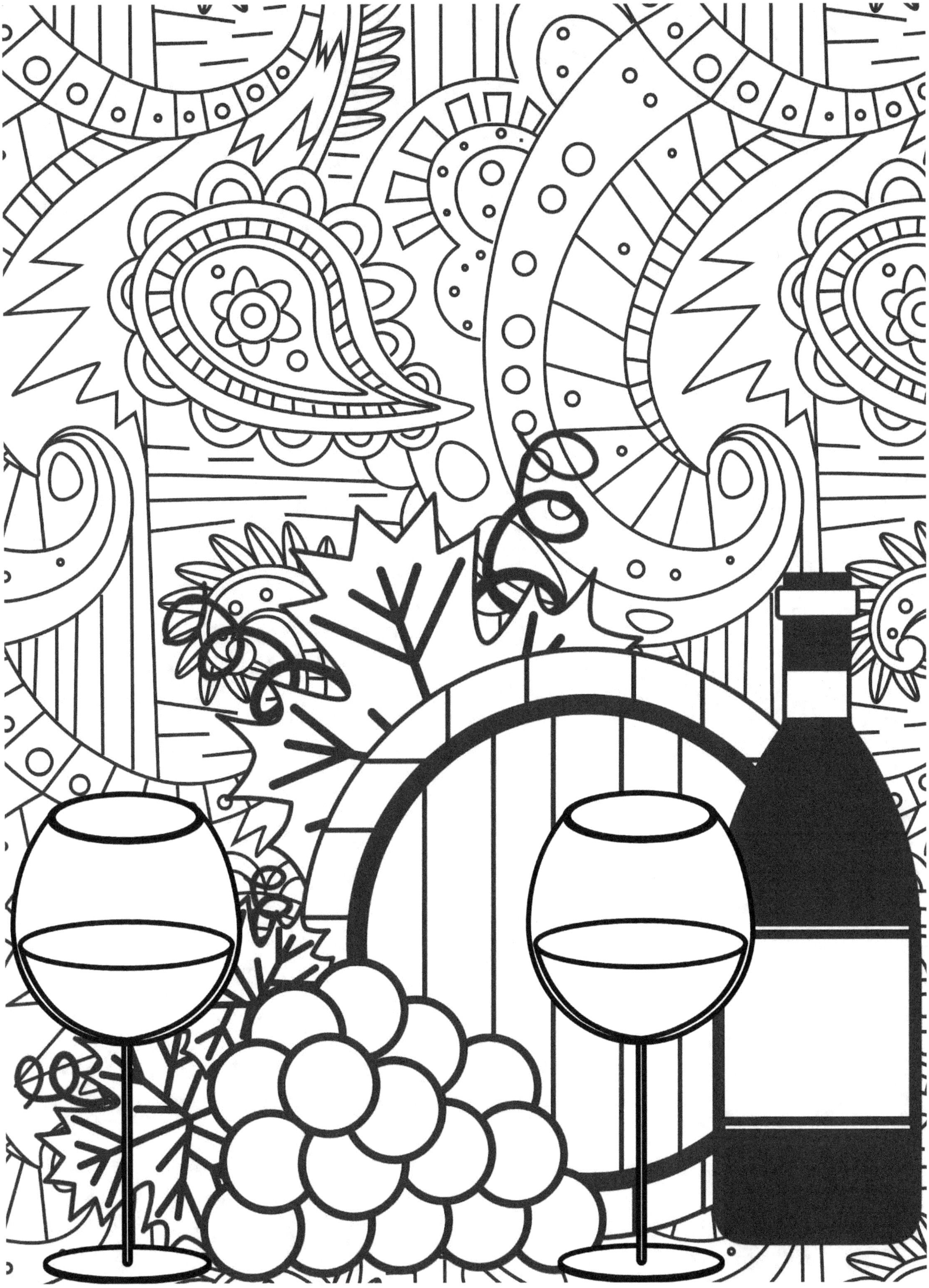

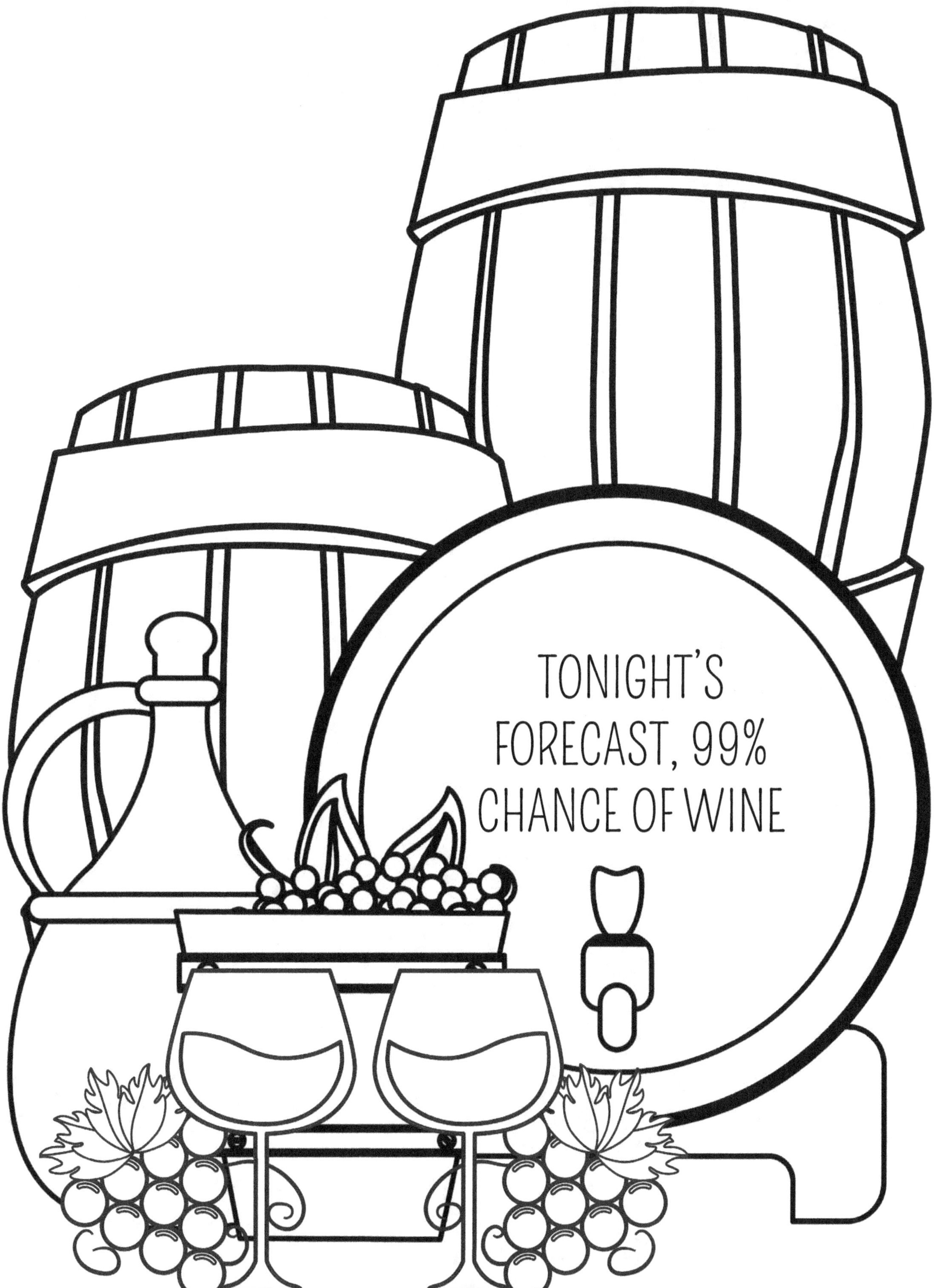
TONIGHT'S
FORECAST, 99%
CHANCE OF WINE

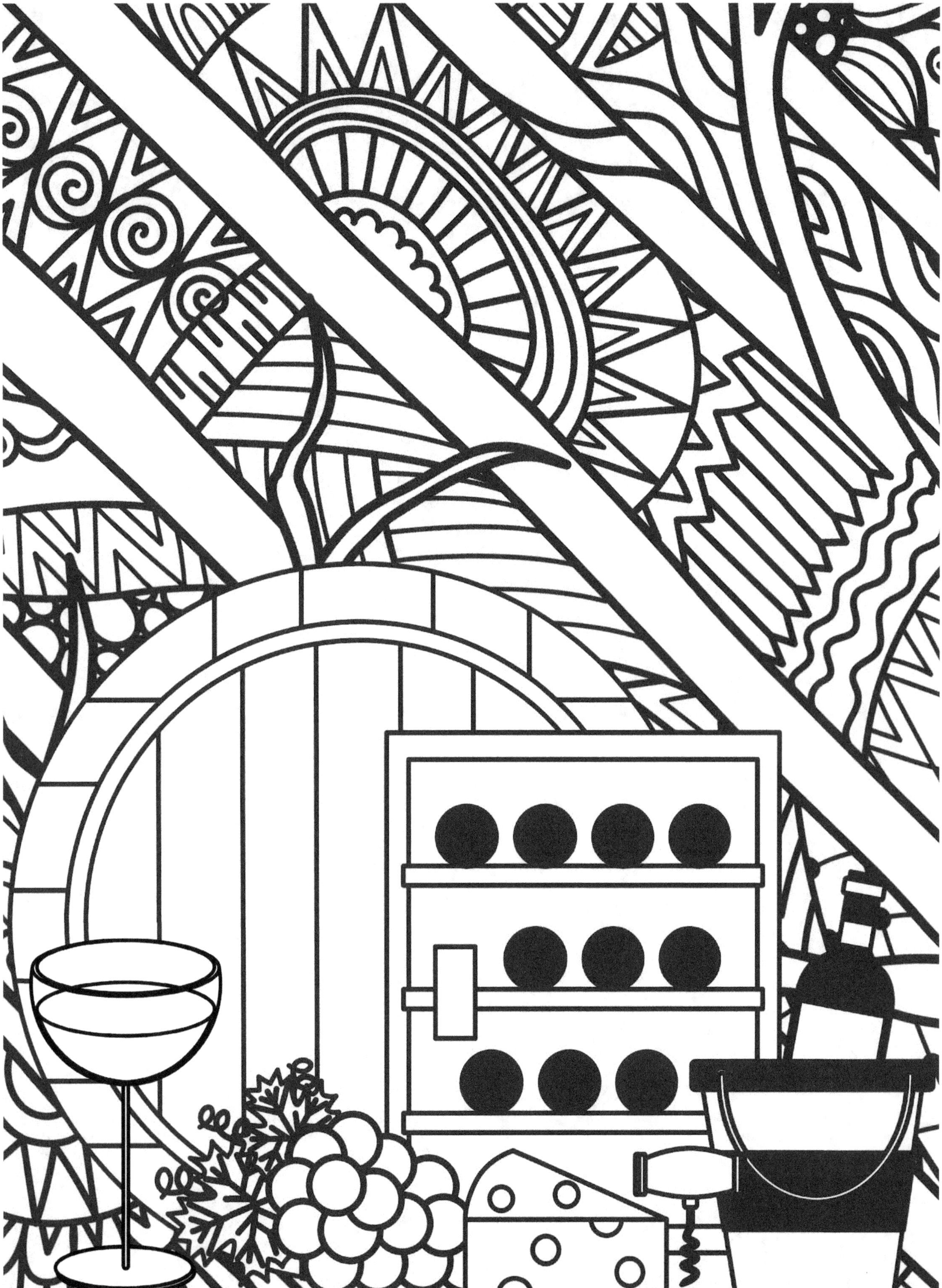

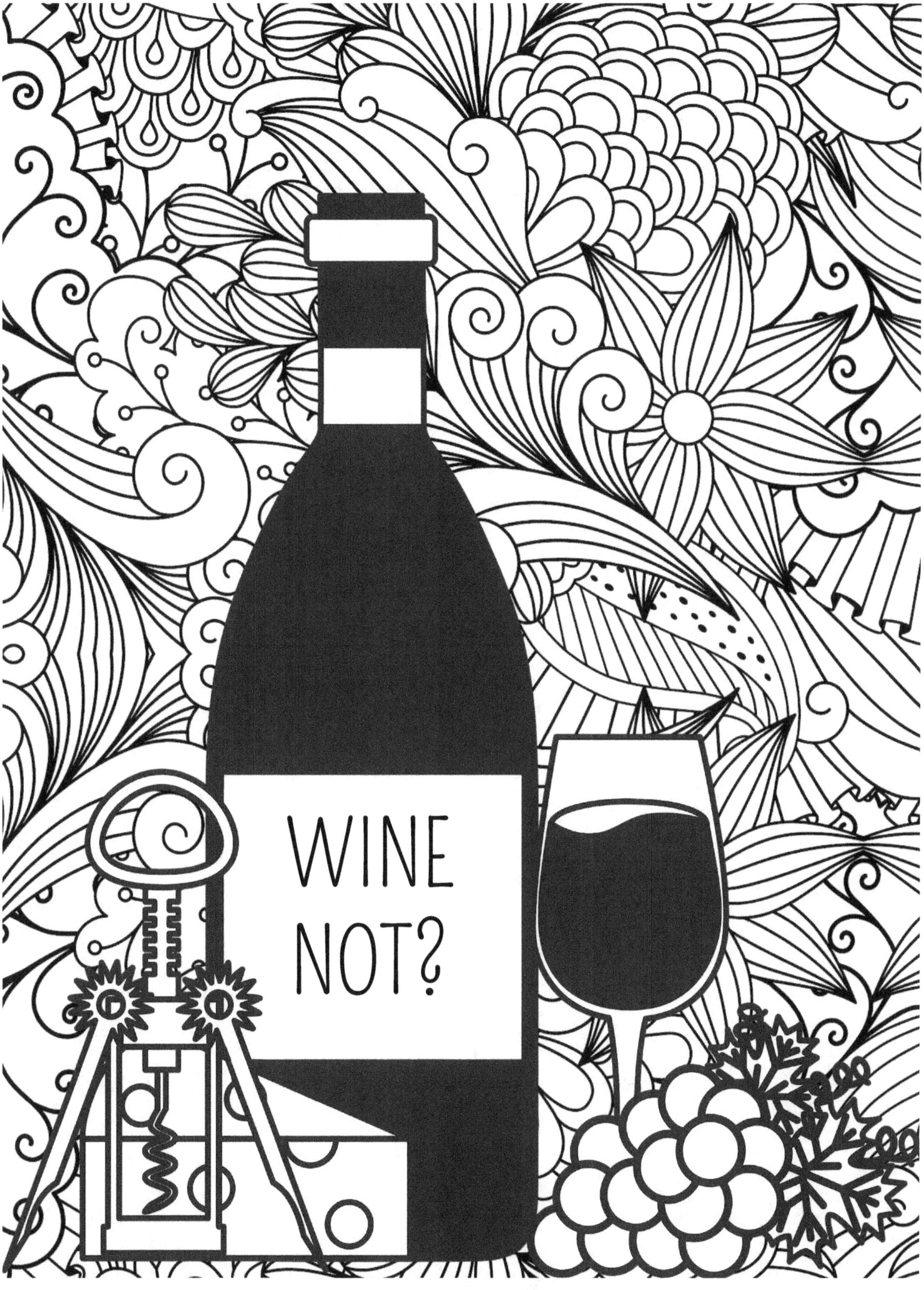
WINE
NOT?

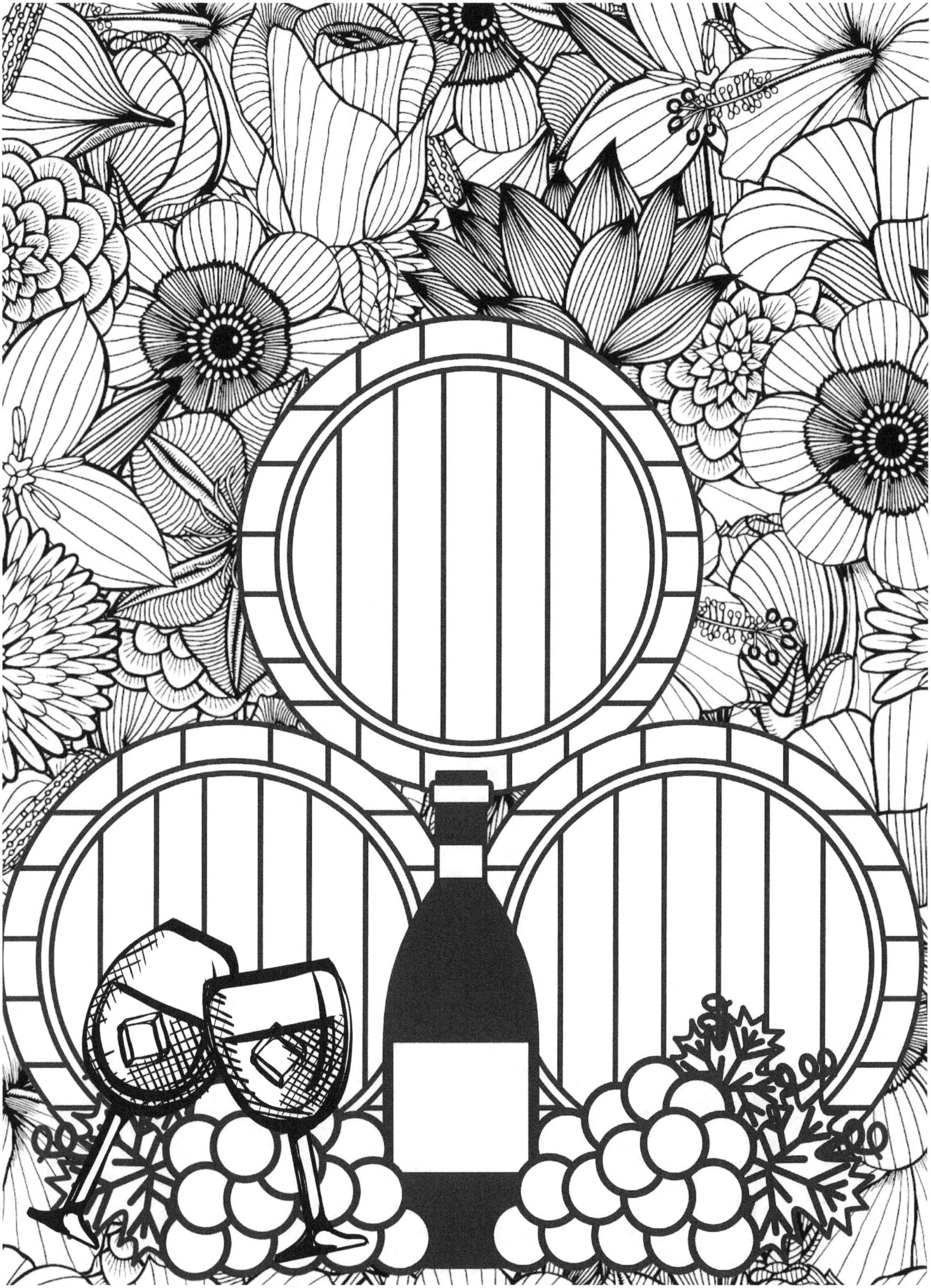

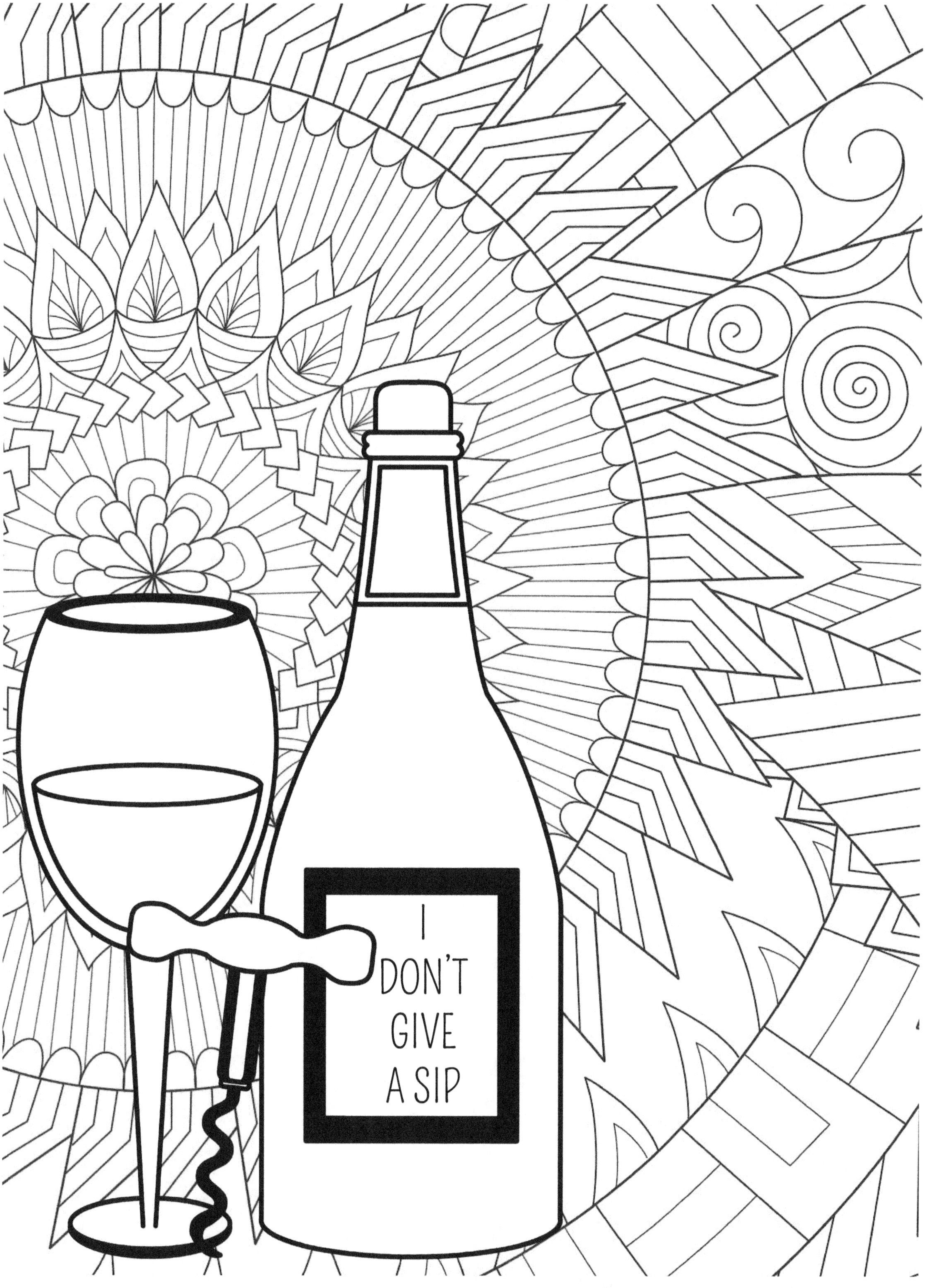
I DON'T GIVE A SIP

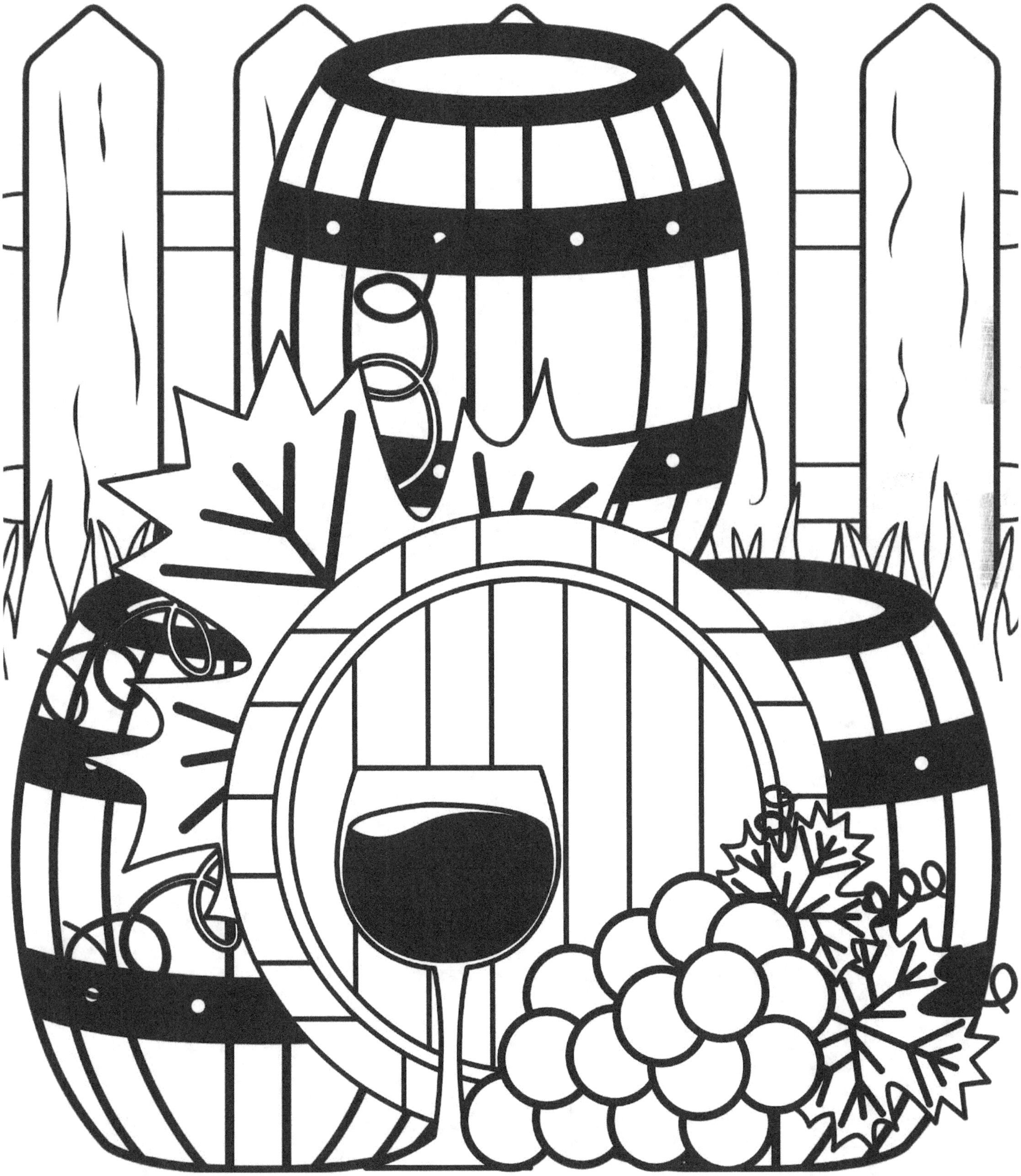

SIP
HAPPENS

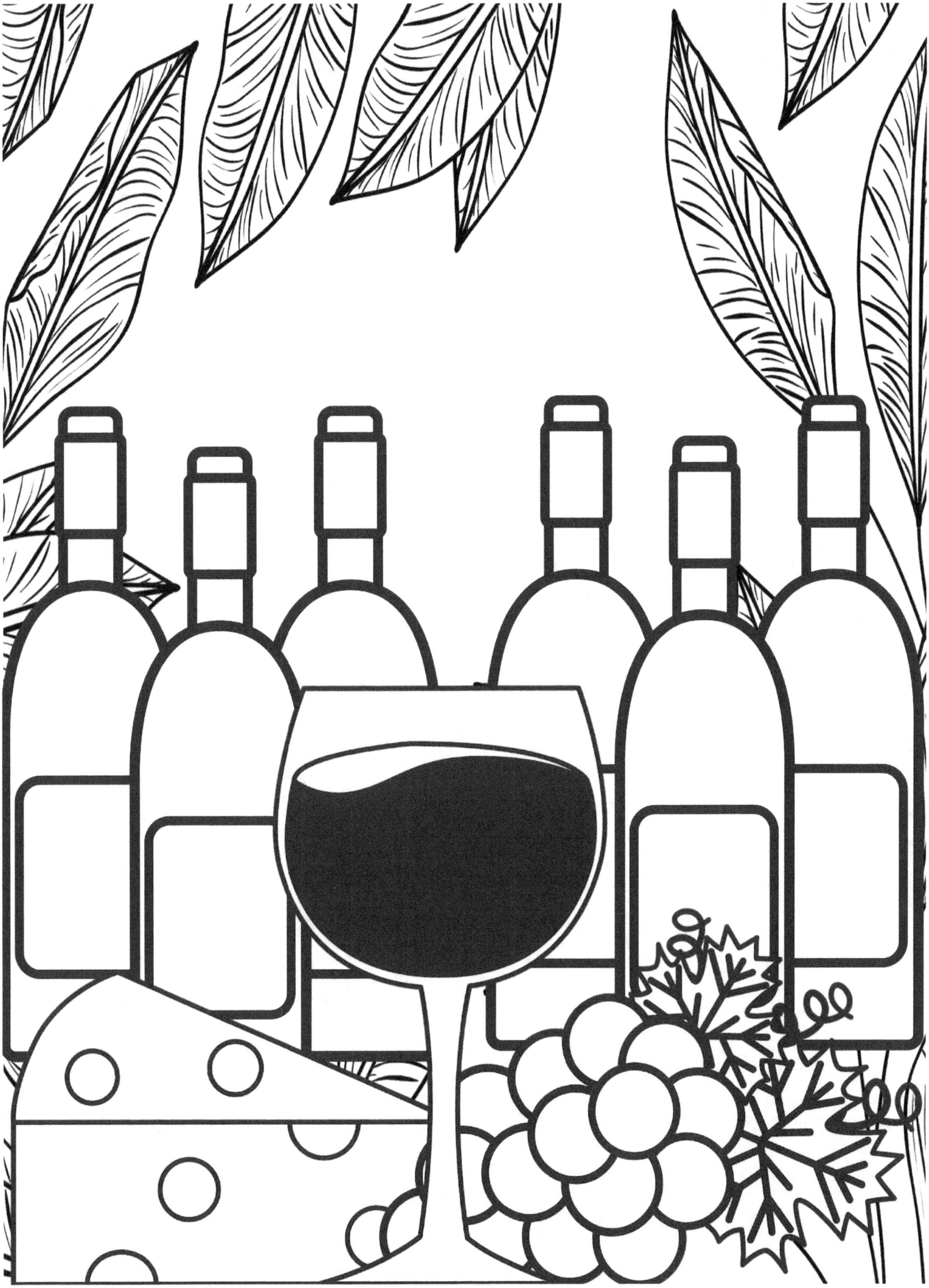

TIME
TO
WINE DOWN

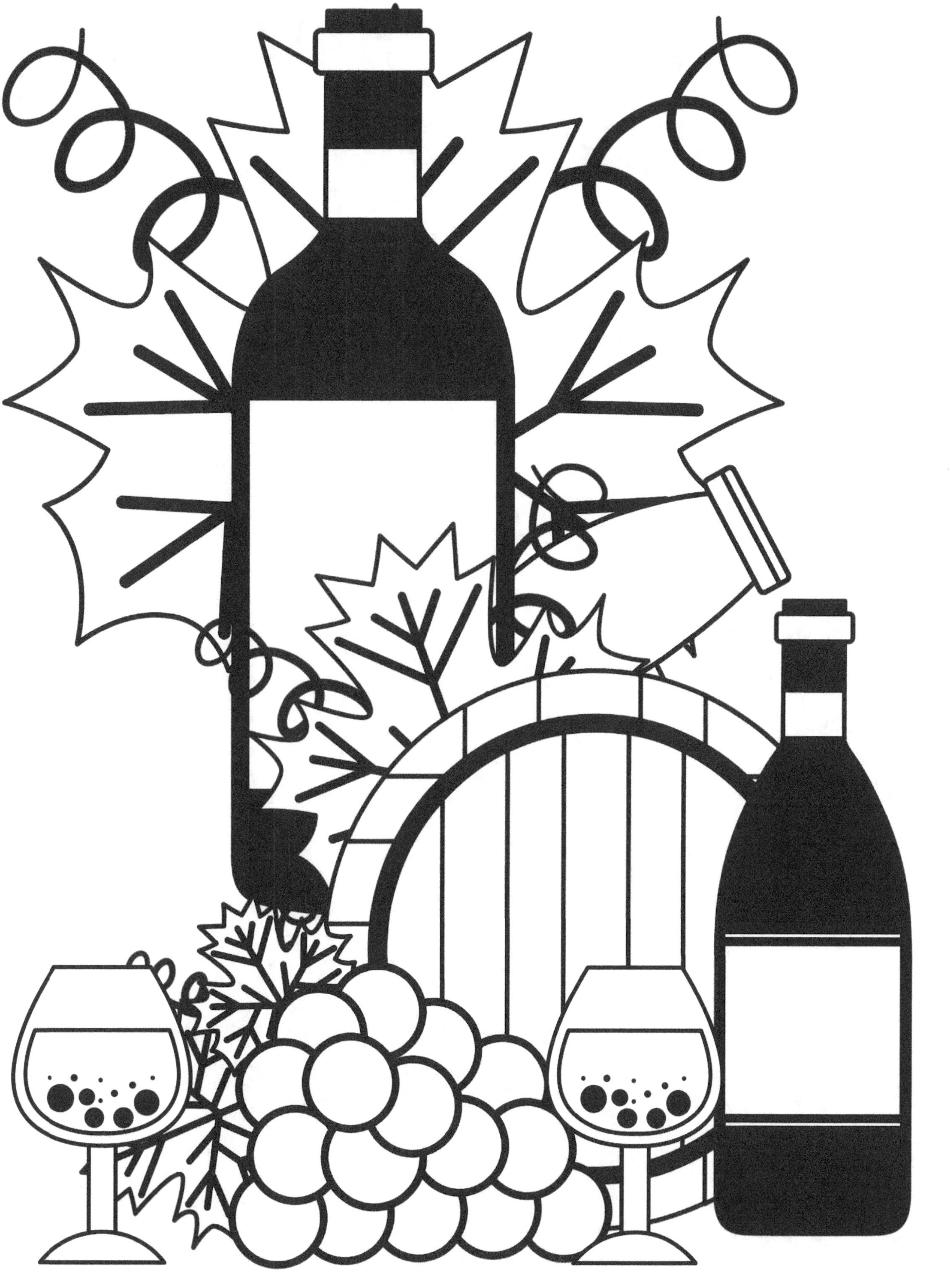

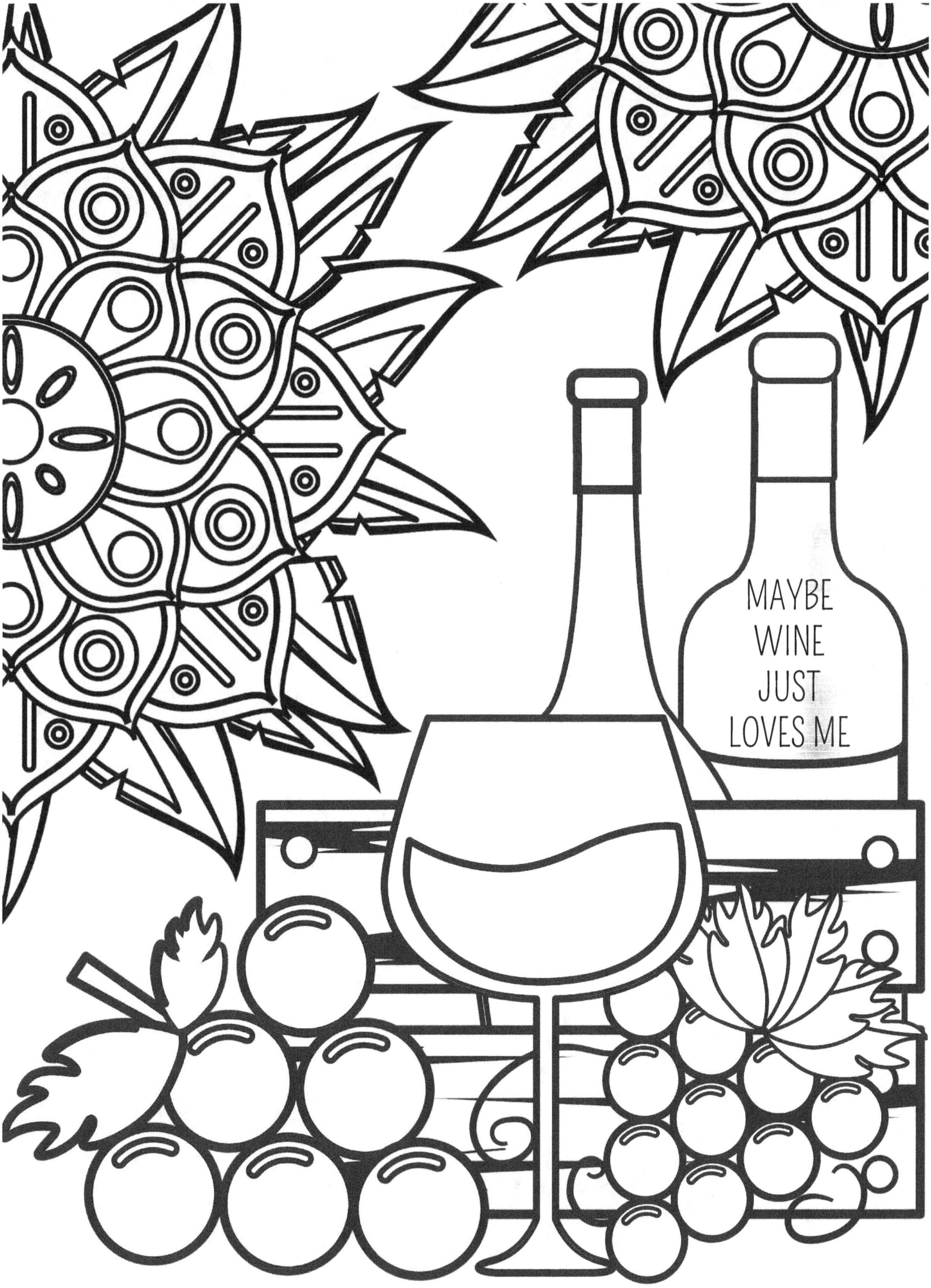
MAYBE
WINE
JUST
LOVES ME

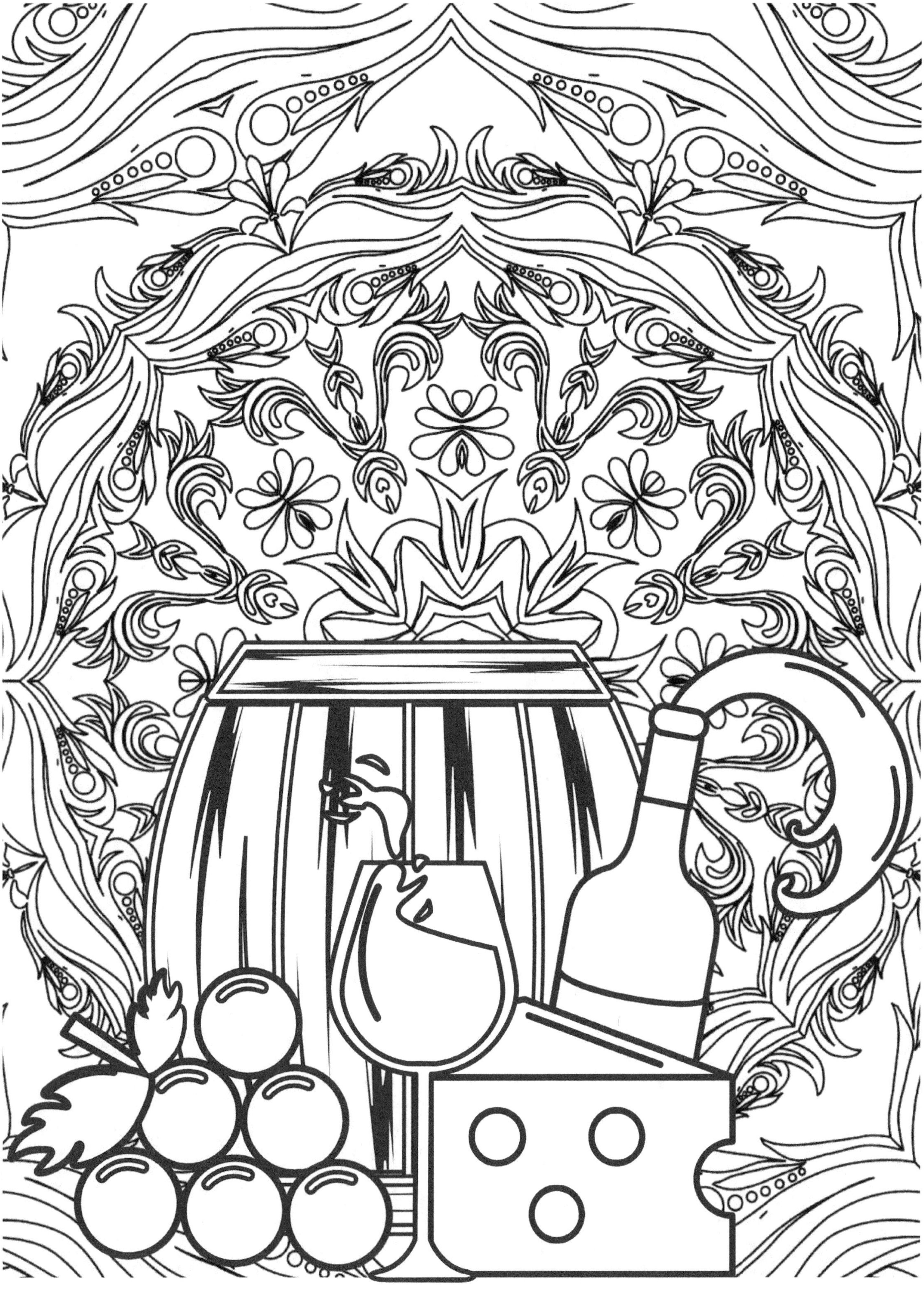

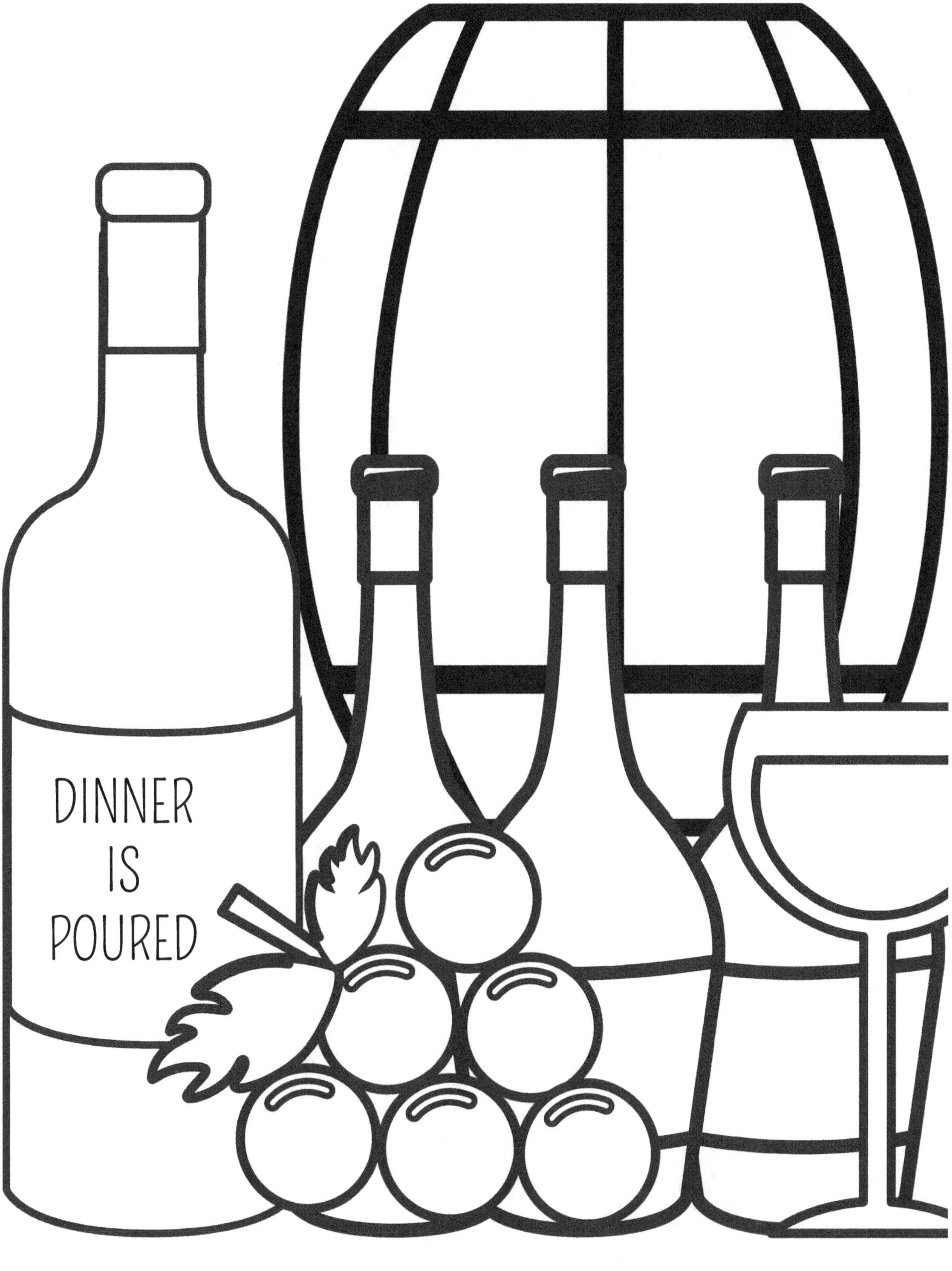
DINNER
IS
POURED

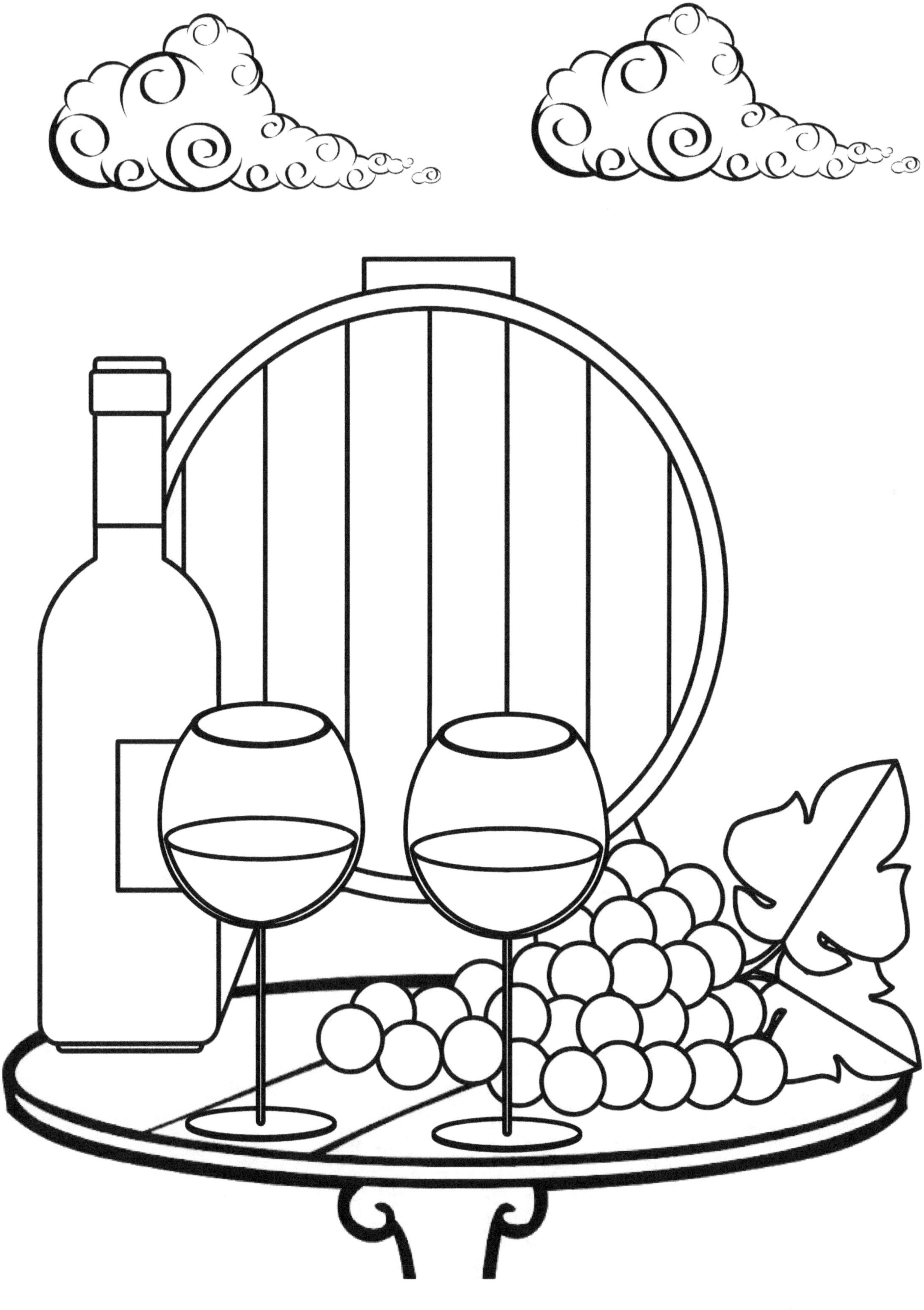

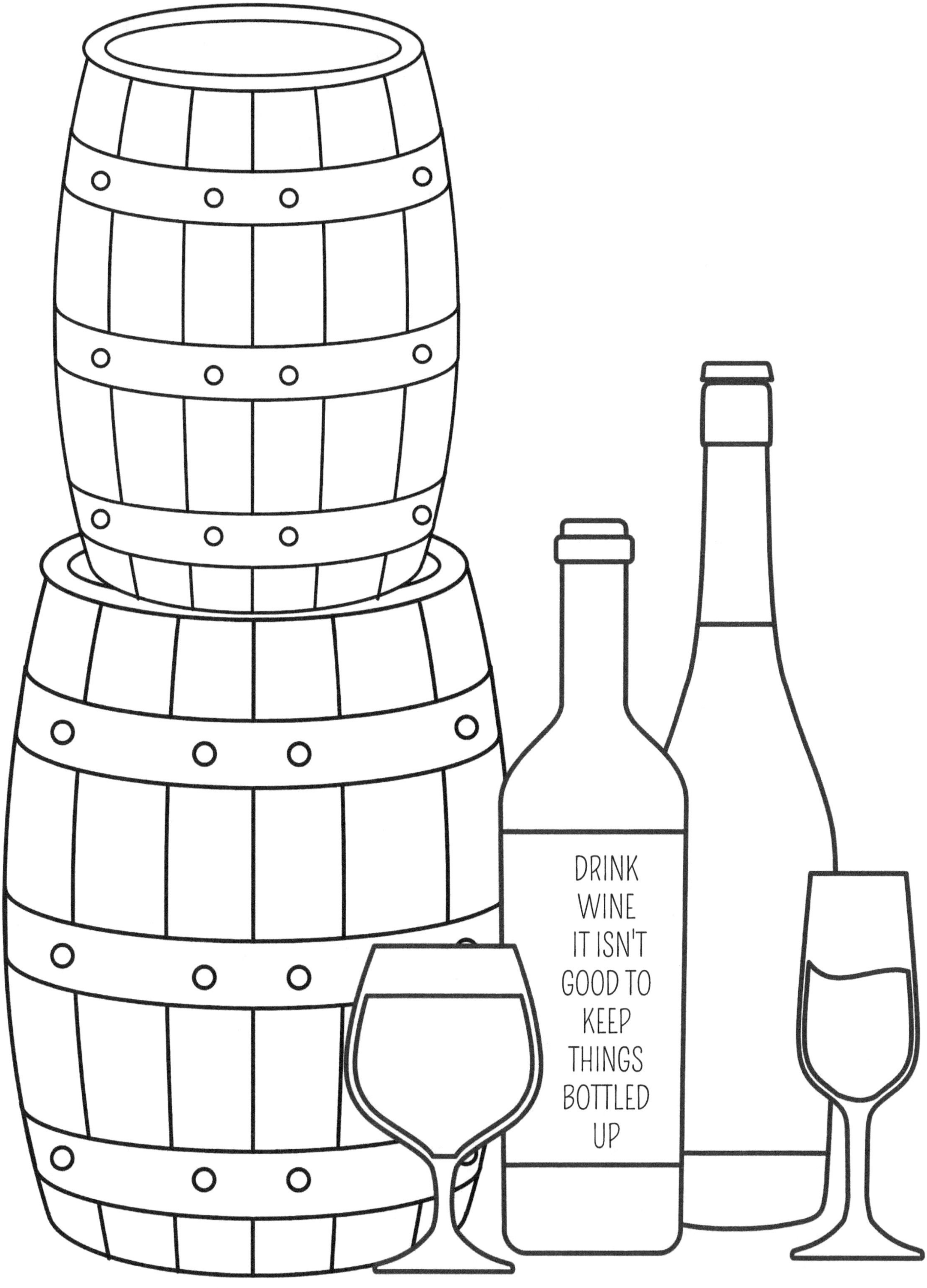
DRINK
WINE
IT ISN'T
GOOD TO
KEEP
THINGS
BOTTLED
UP

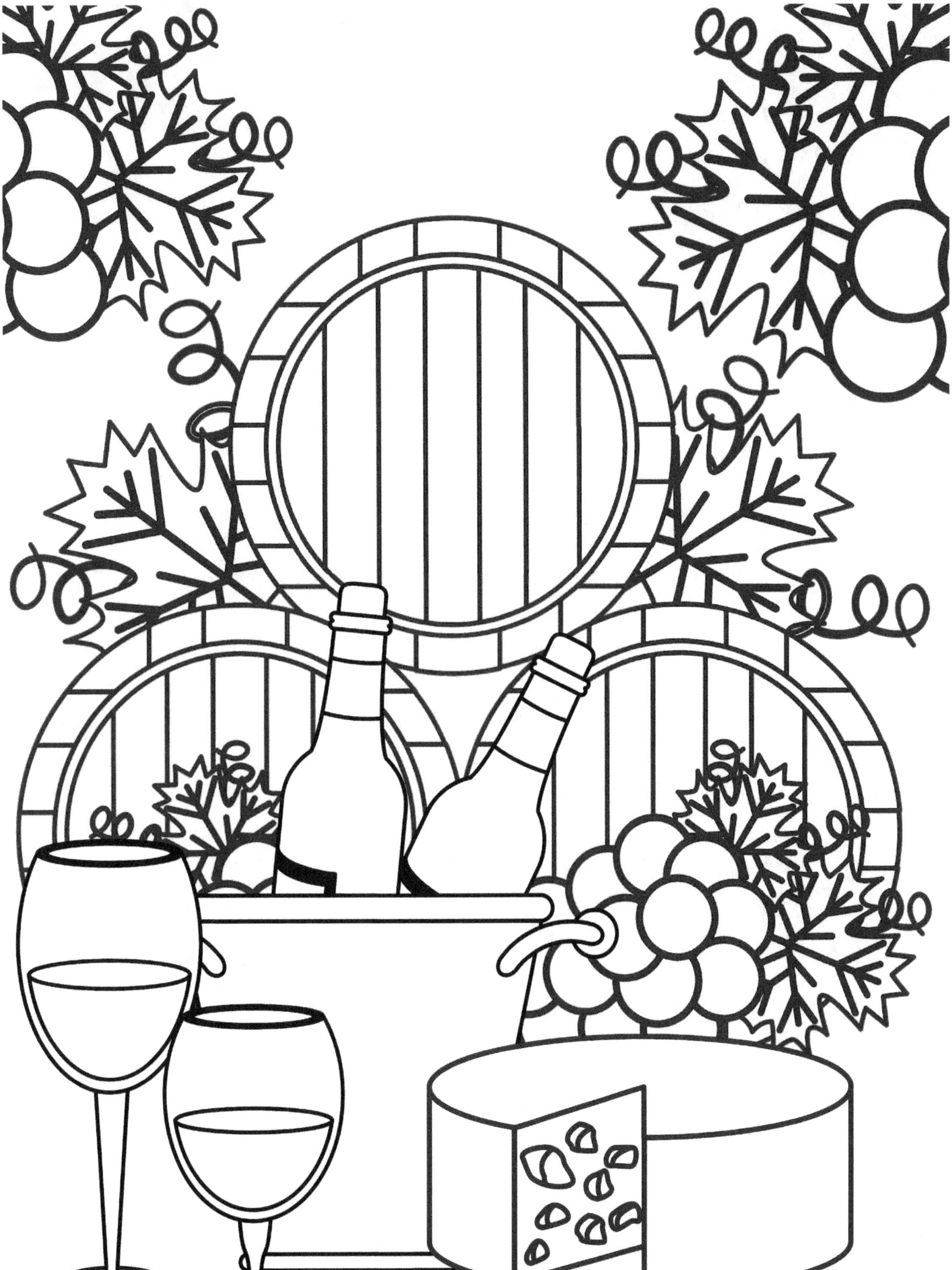

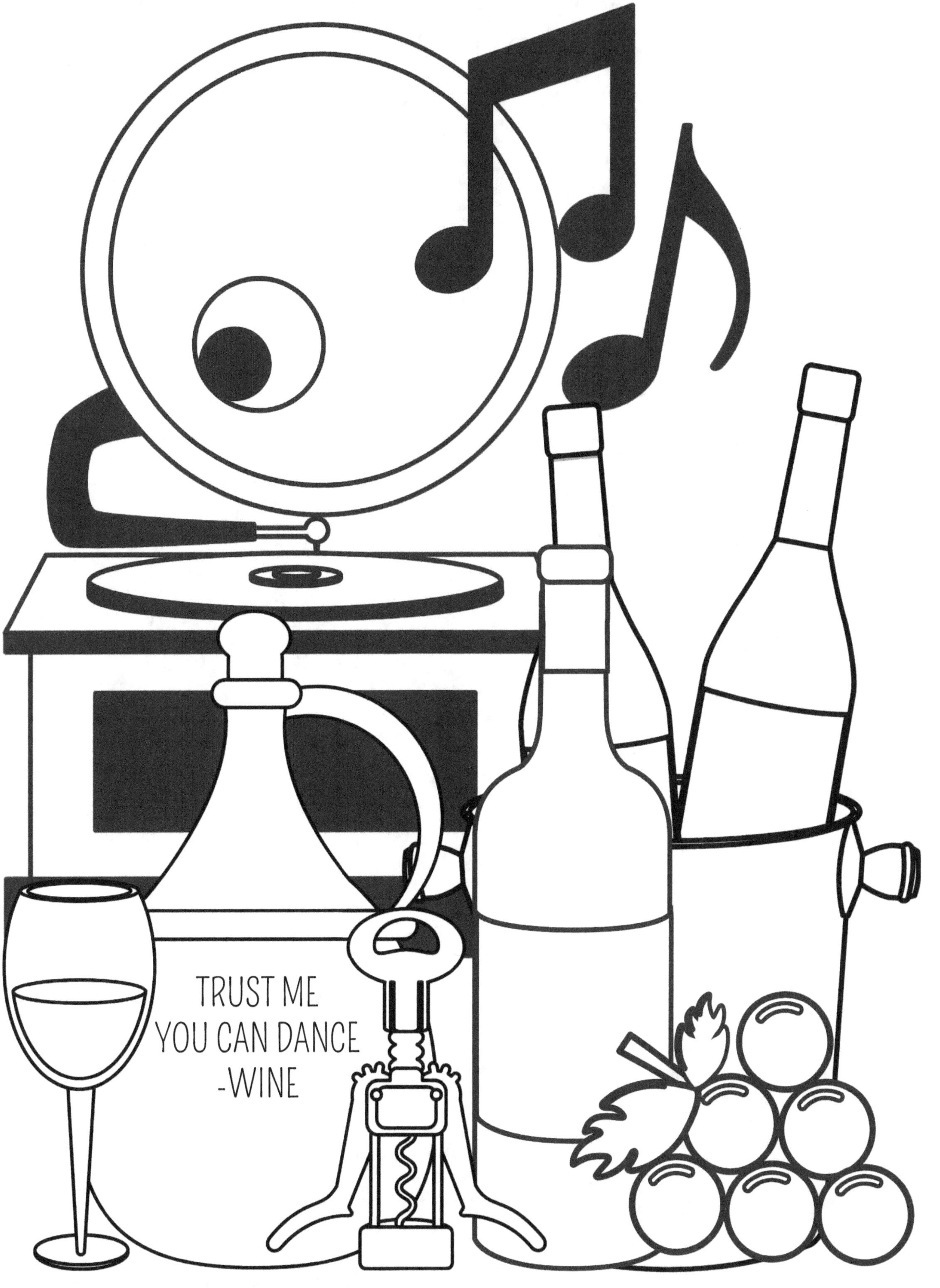
TRUST ME
YOU CAN DANCE
-WINE

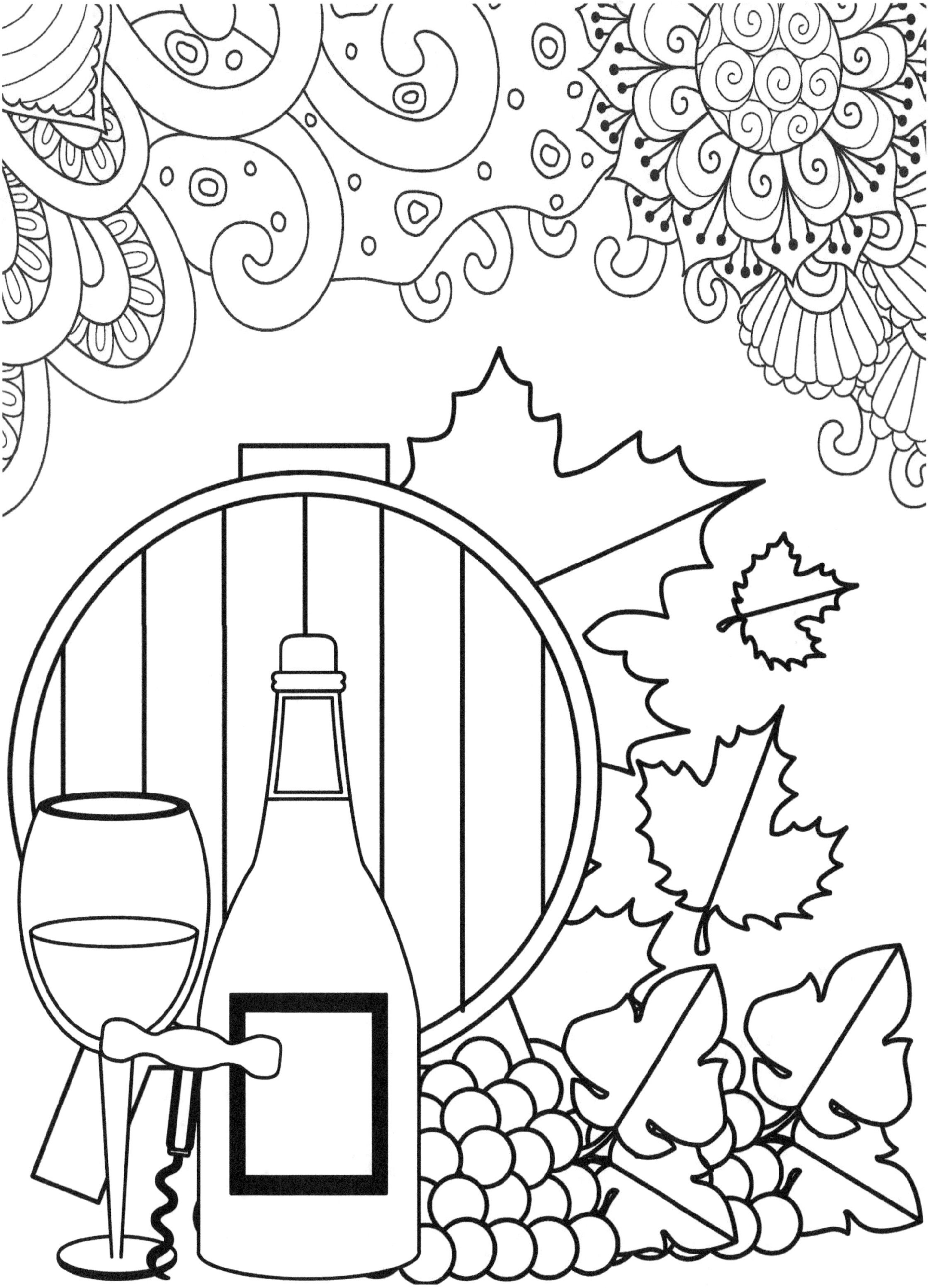

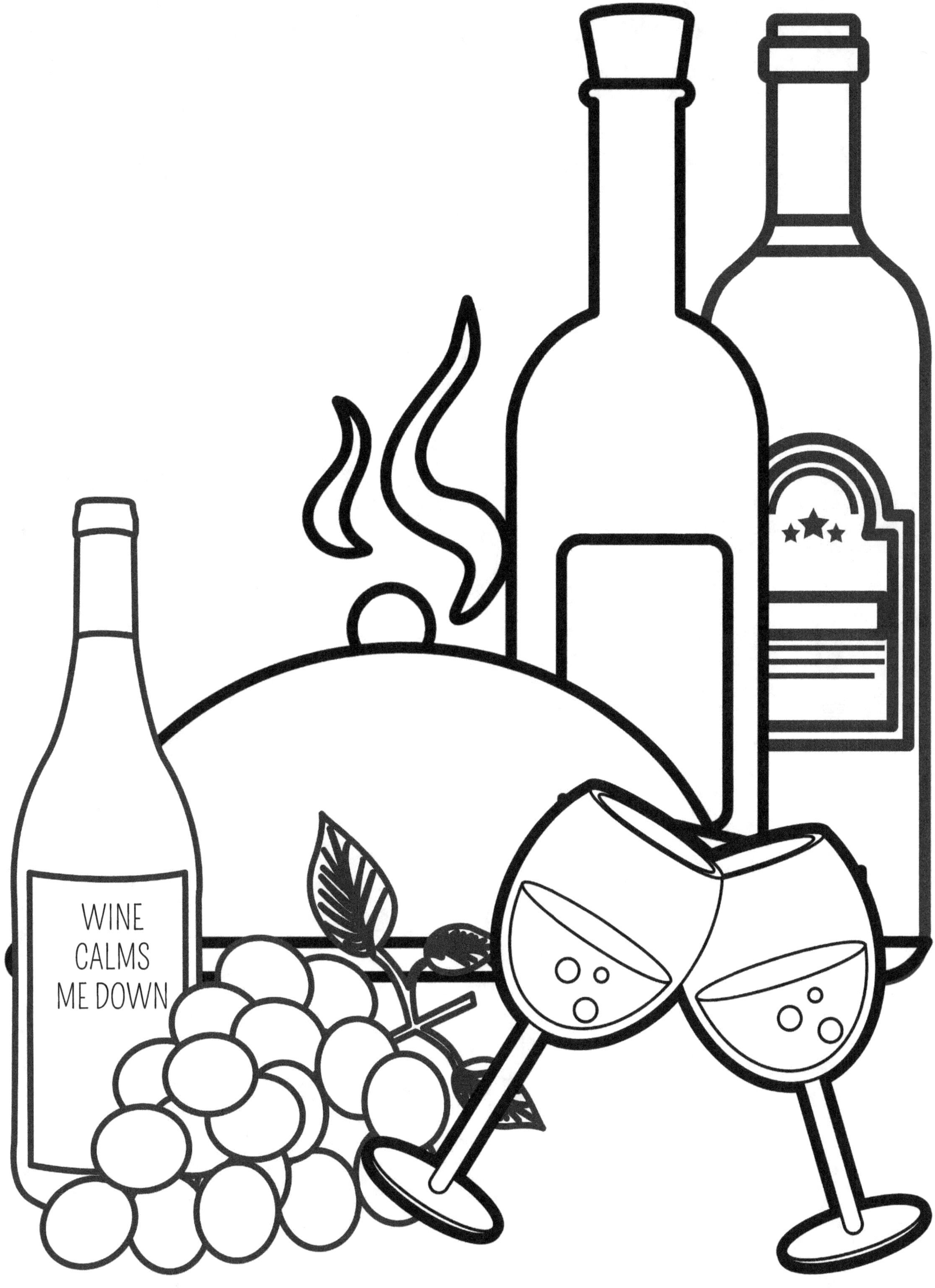
WINE
CALMS
ME DOWN

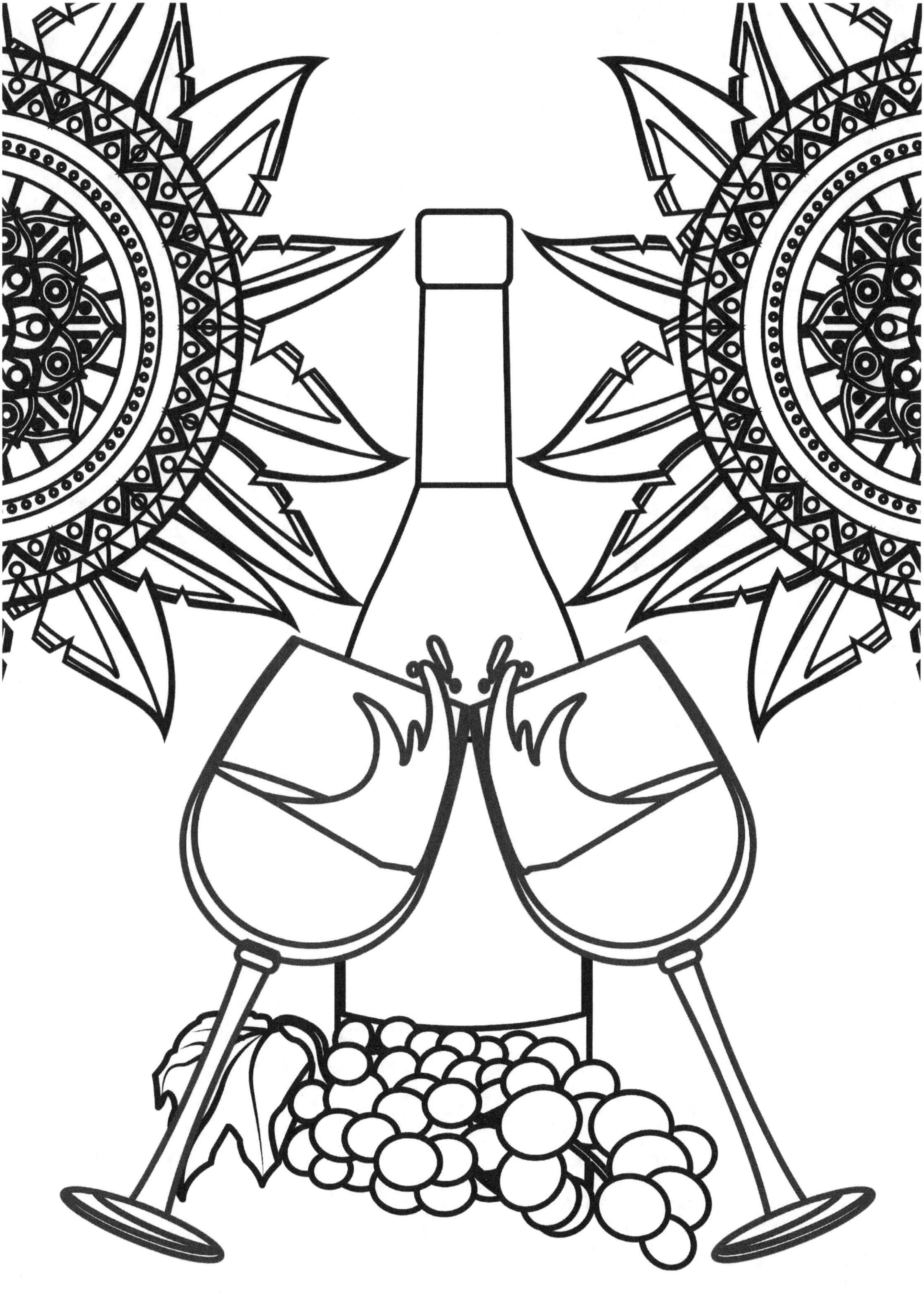

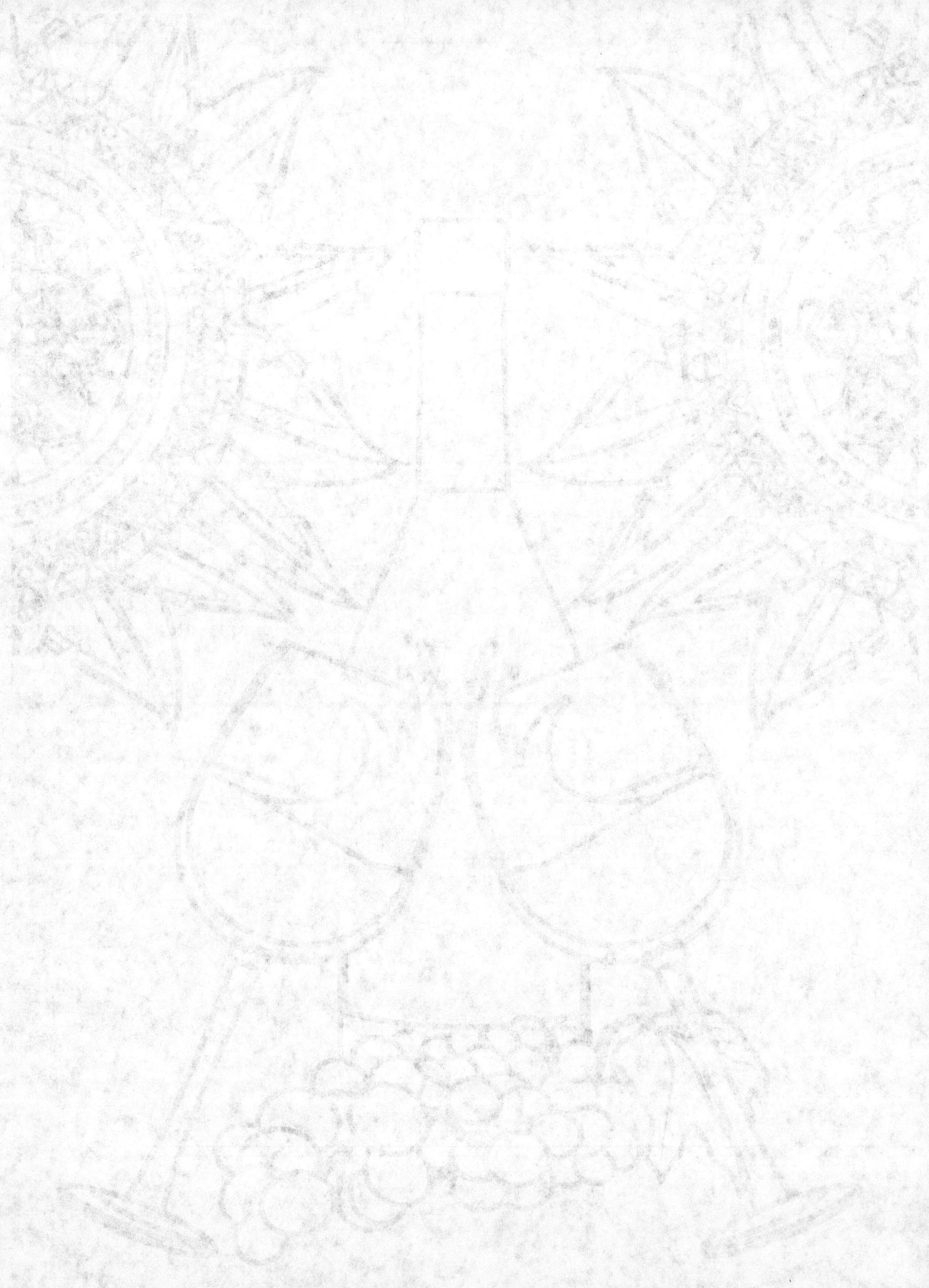

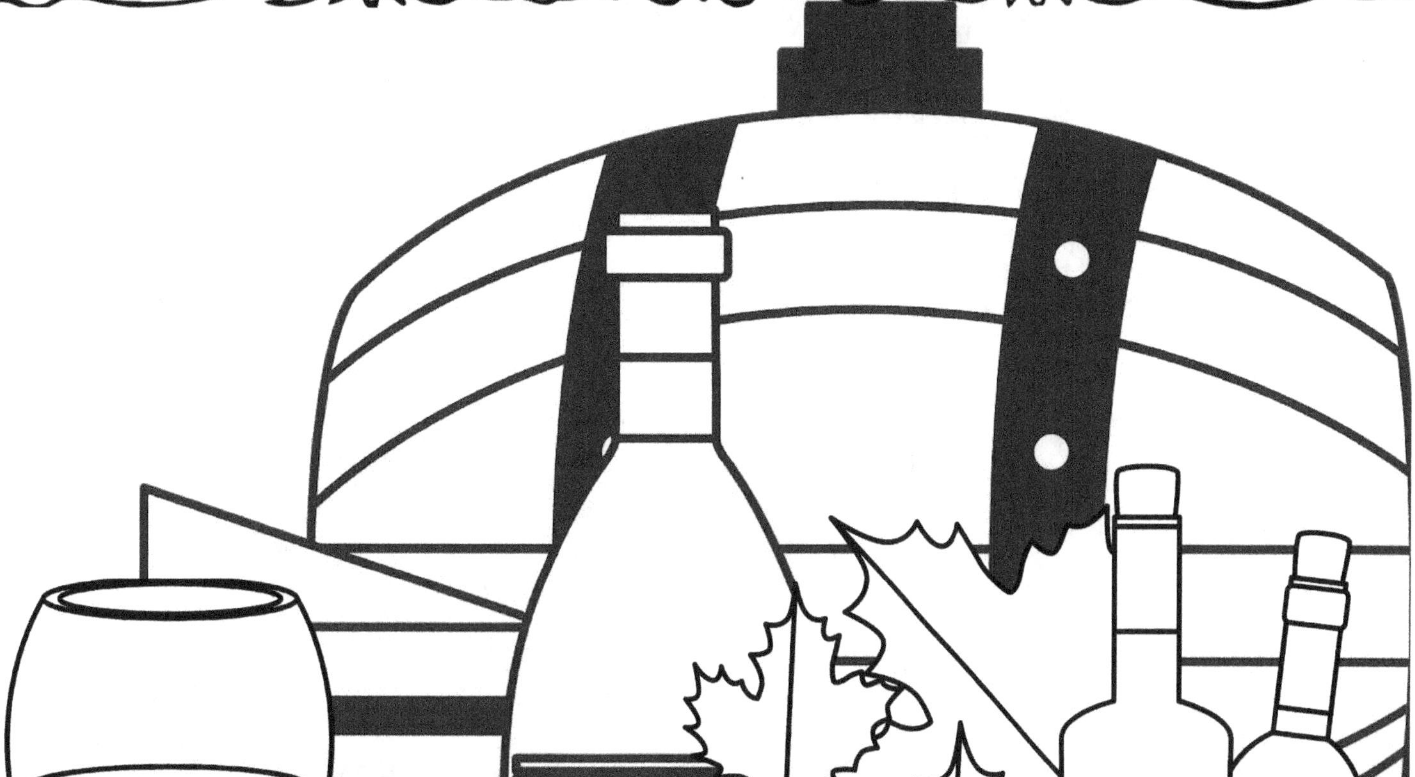
WINE
IS
THE
BEST
CURE

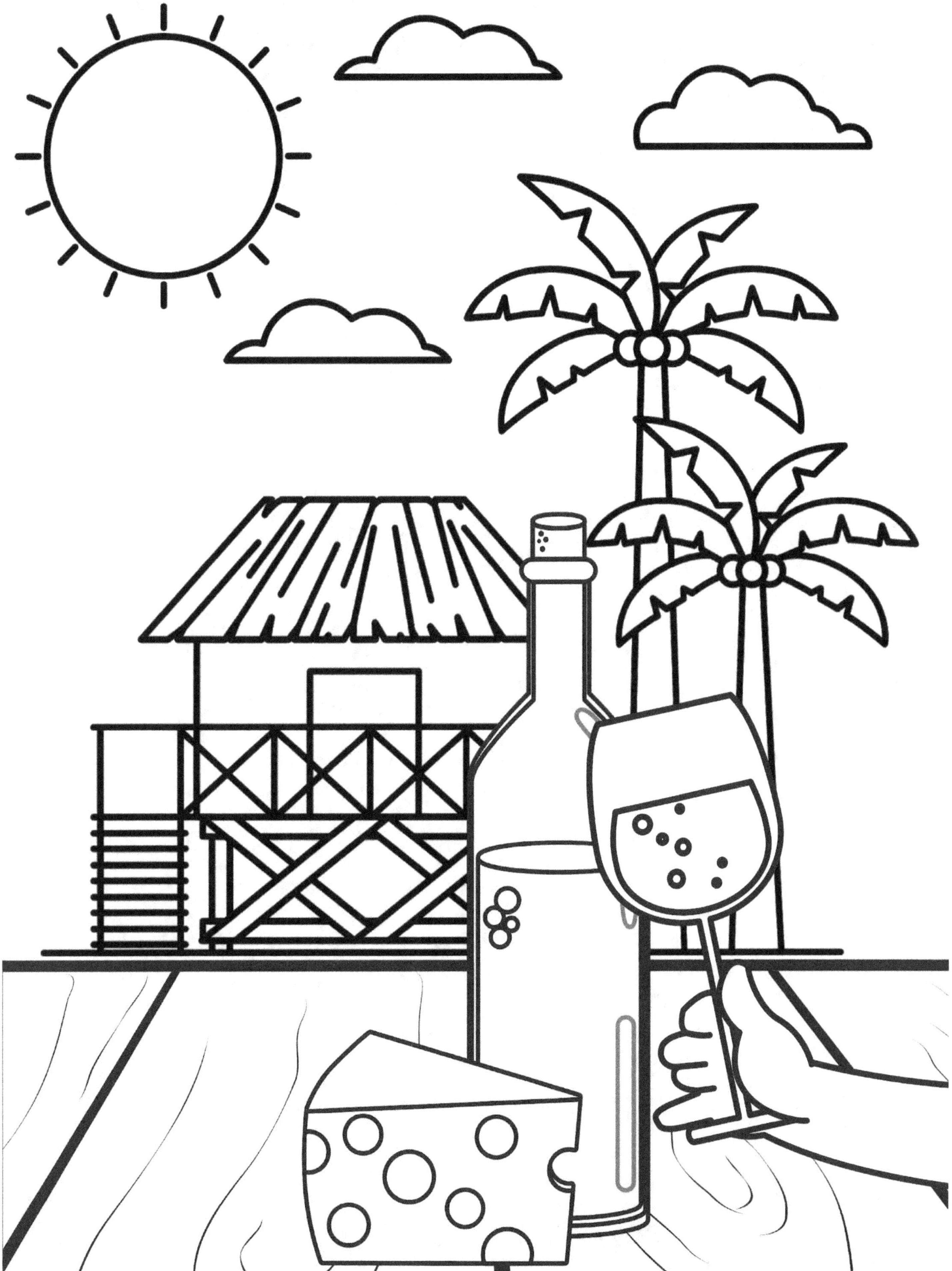

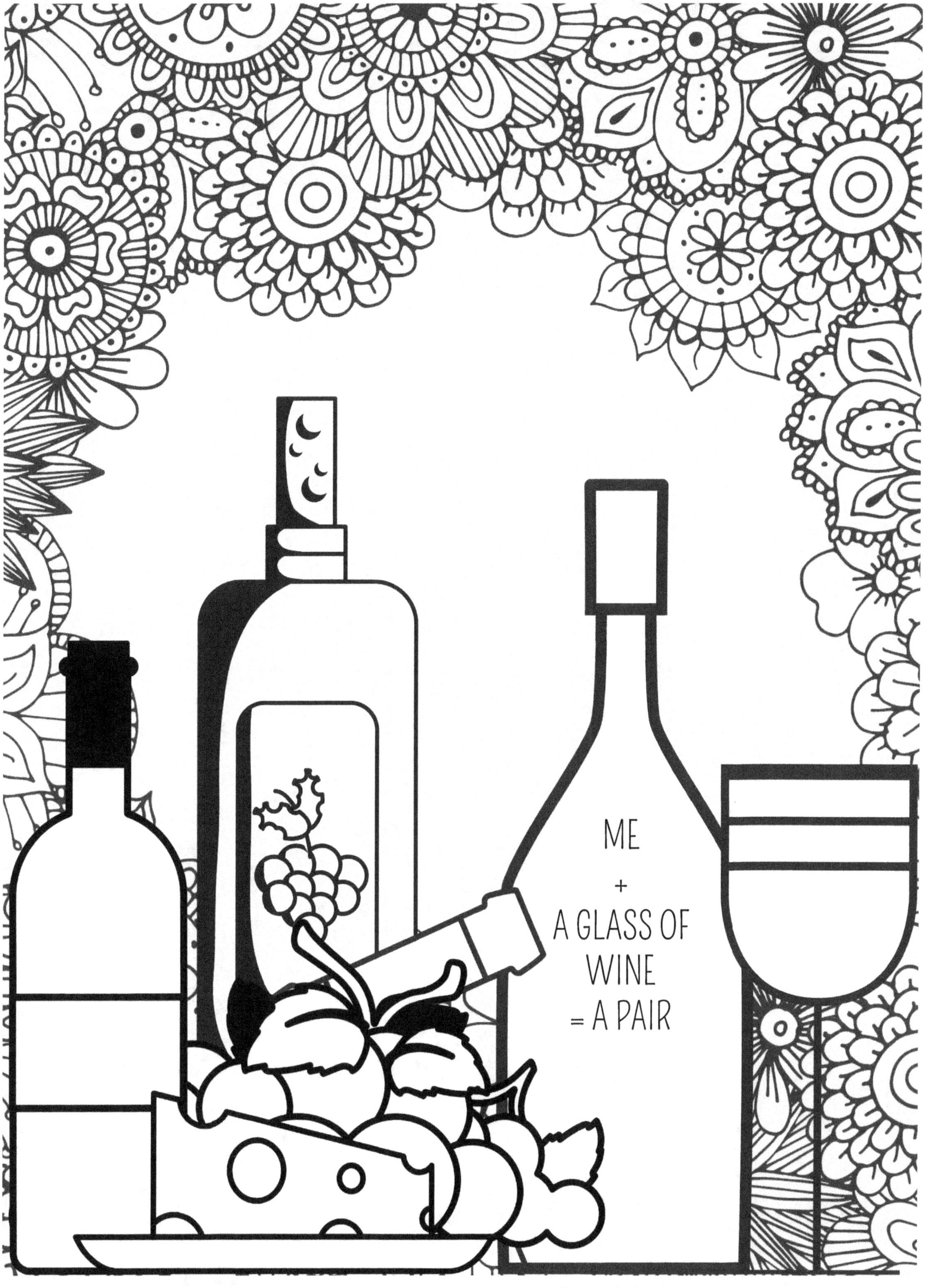
ME
+
A GLASS OF
WINE
= A PAIR

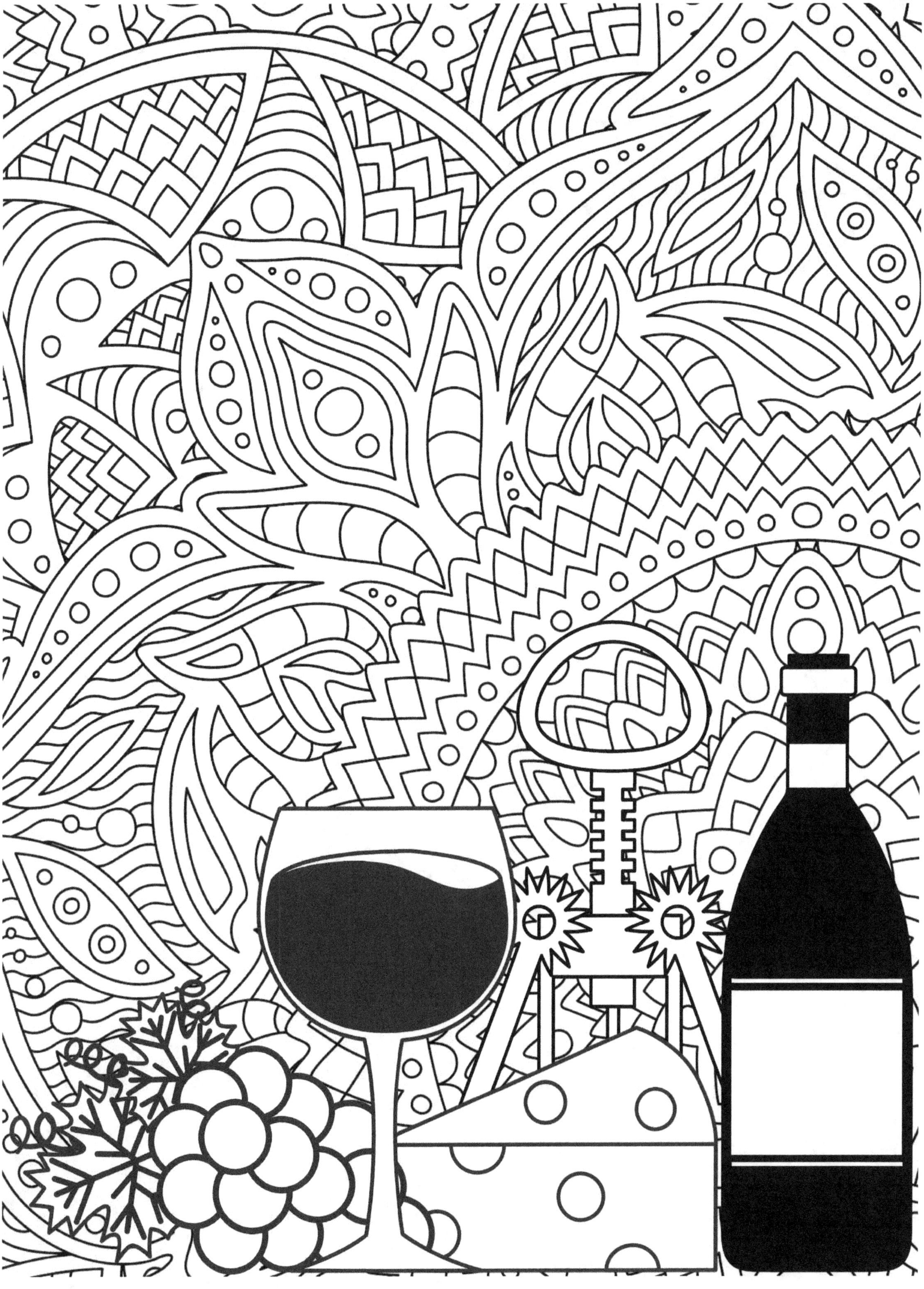

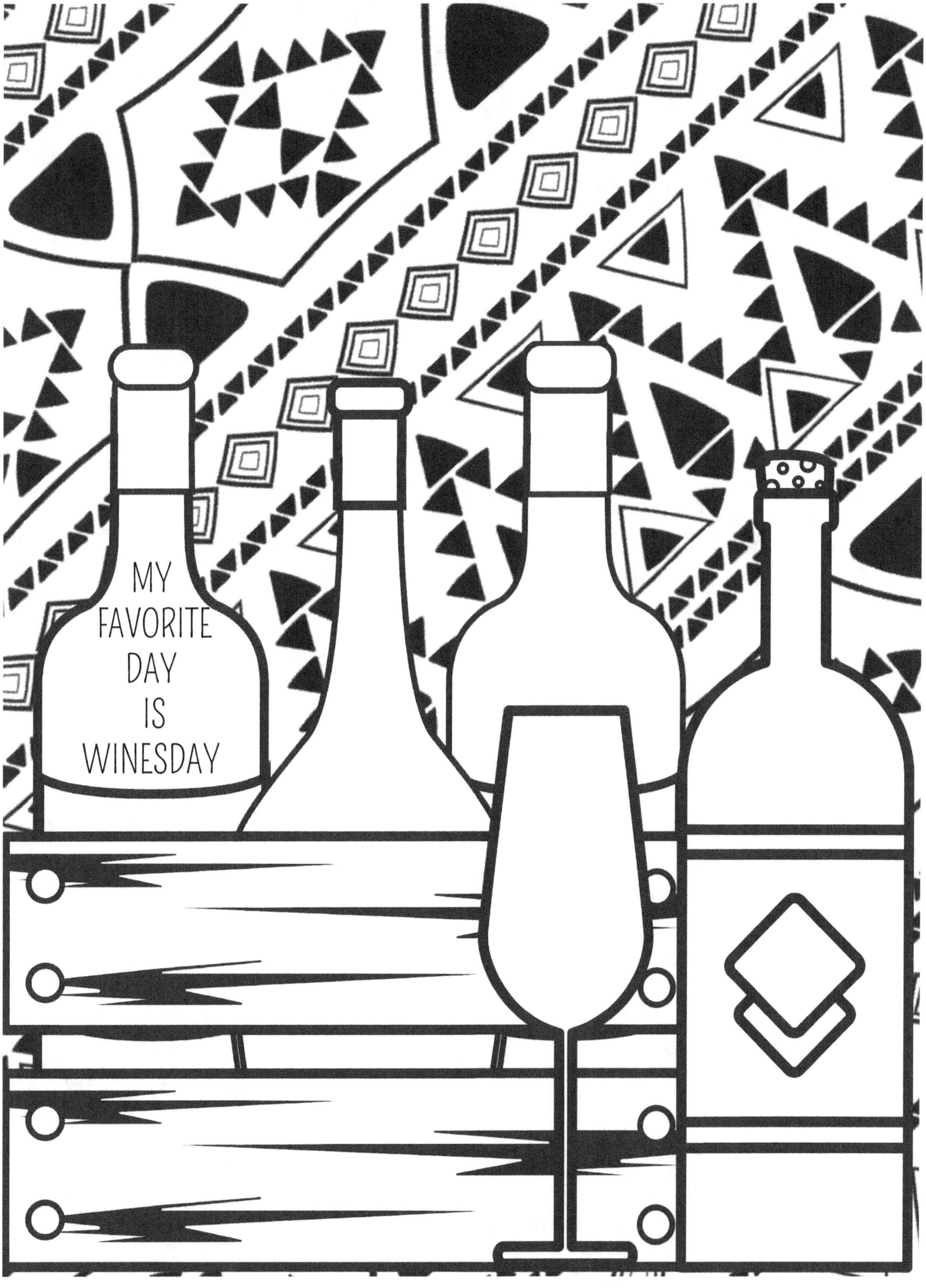
MY
FAVORITE
DAY
IS
WINESDAY

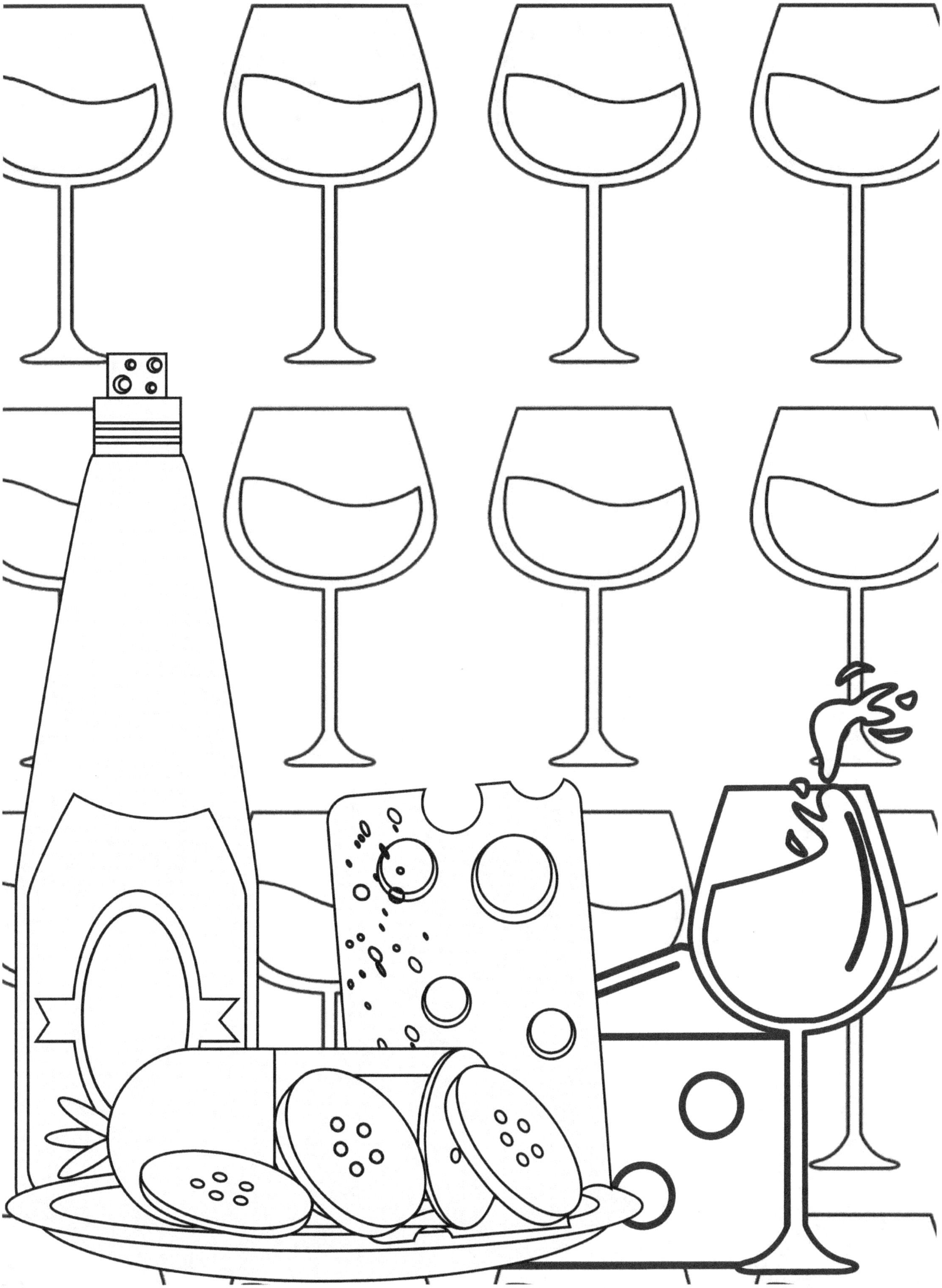

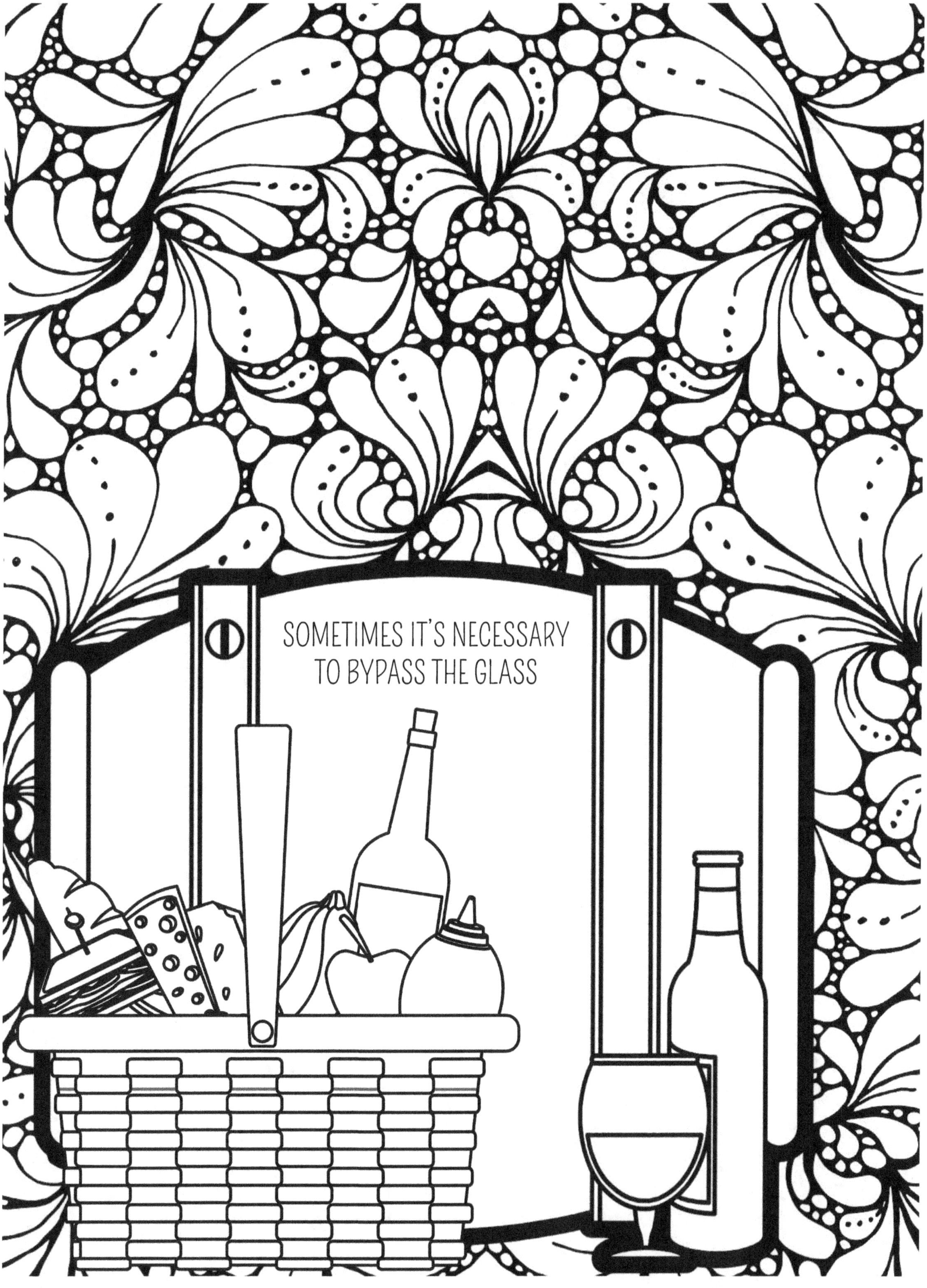
SOMETIMES IT'S NECESSARY
TO BYPASS THE GLASS

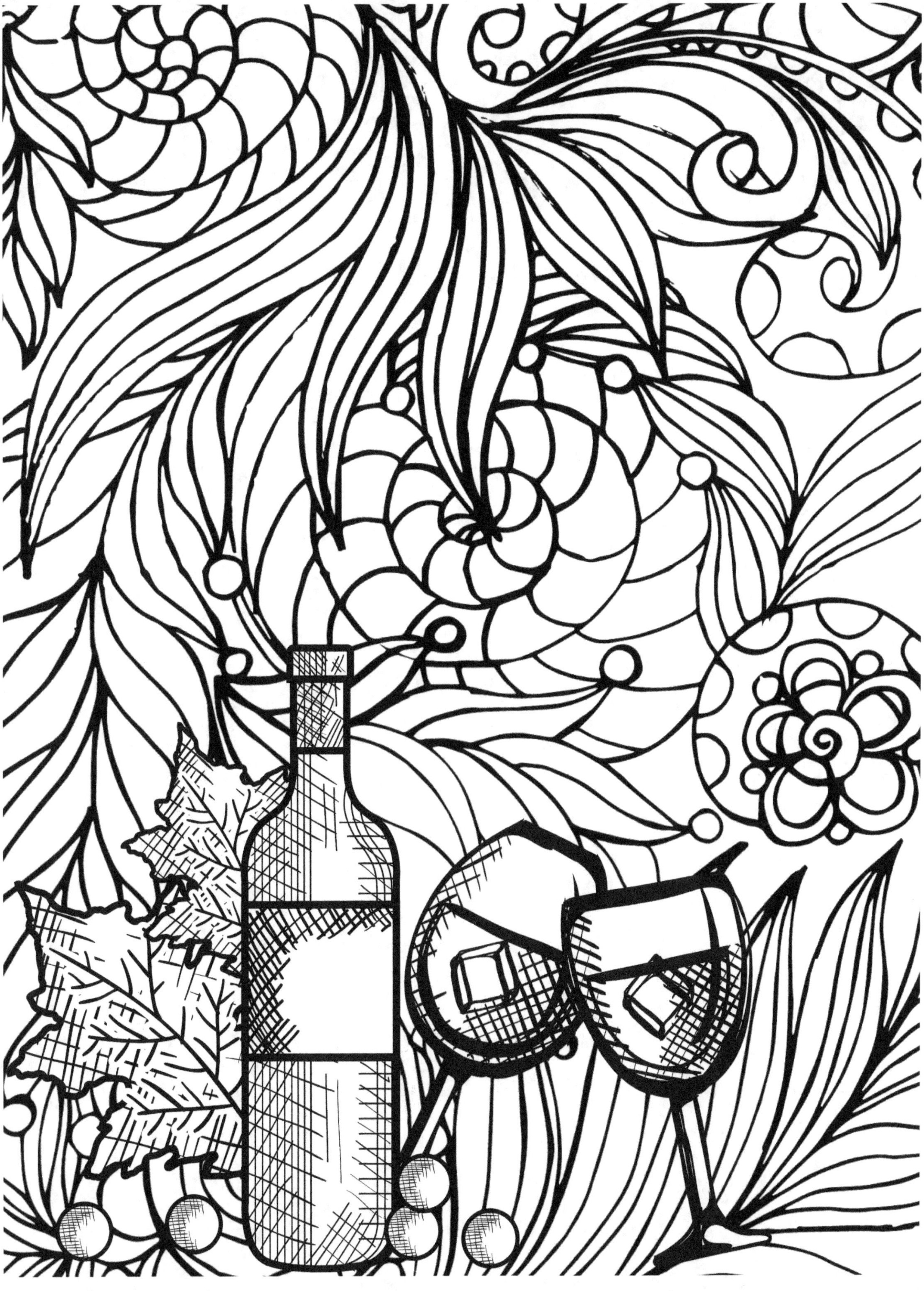

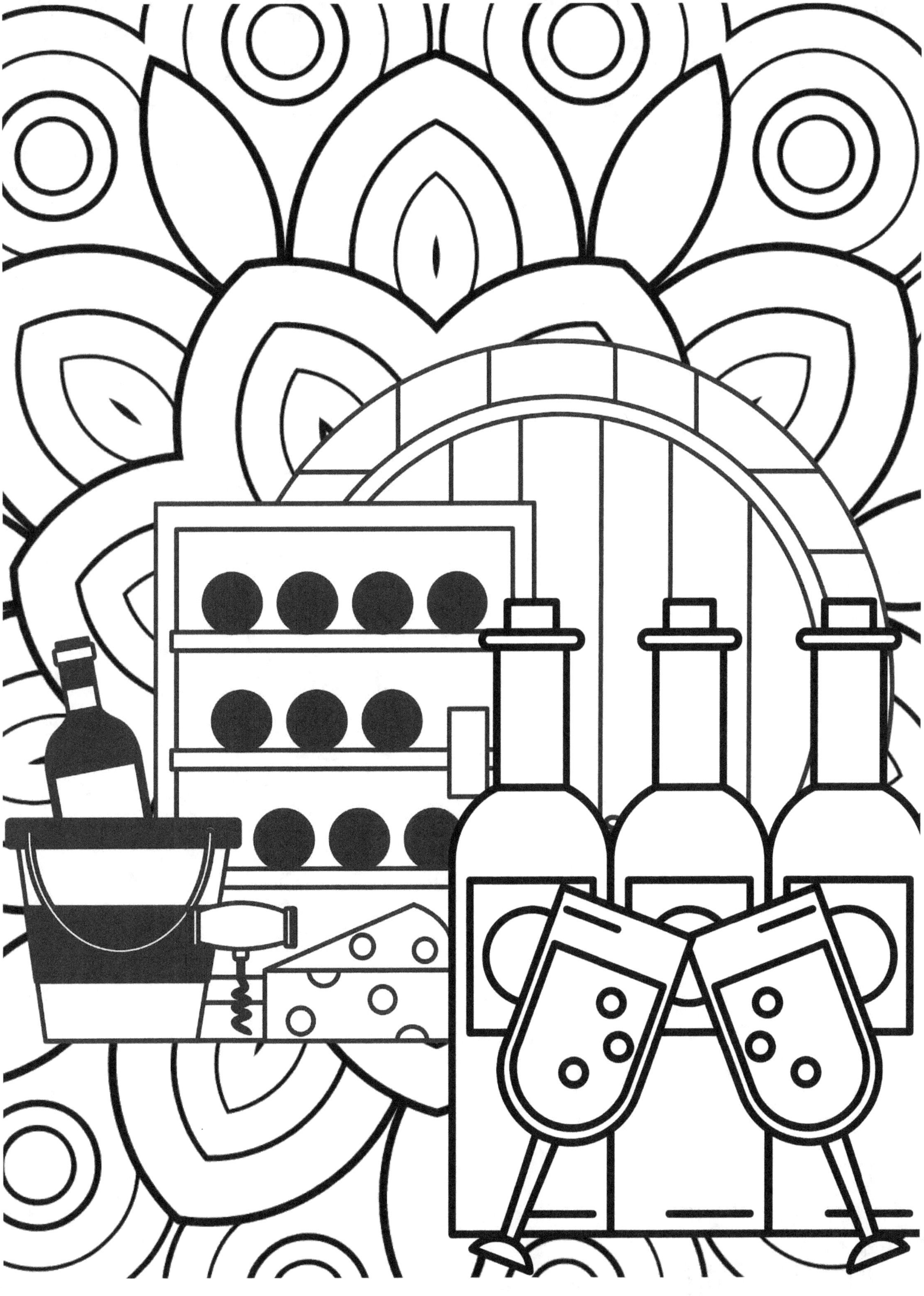

www.ingramcontent.com/pod-product-compliance
Lightning Source LLC
Chambersburg PA
CBHW080519220526
45465CB00006B/2538
9798676620127